THE BITEBACK DICTIONARY OF
HUMOROUS LITERARY QUOTATIONS

The Biteback Dictionary of

HUMOROUS
LITERARY
QUOTATIONS

—— *Fred Metcalf* ——

Biteback Publishing

First published in Great Britain in 2013 by
Biteback Publishing Ltd
Westminster Tower
3 Albert Embankment
London SE1 7SP
Copyright © Fred Metcalf 2013

ISBN 978-1-84954-226-5

10 9 8 7 6 5 4 3 2 1

A CIP catalogue record for this book is available from the British Library.

Set in Sabon

Printed and bound in Great Britain by
CPI Group (UK) Ltd, Croydon CR0 4YY

CONTENTS

INTRODUCTION

There are times in every man's experience when some sudden widening of the boundaries of his knowledge, some vision of hitherto untried and unrealised possibilities, has come through the pages of a book and seemed to bring with it new life and the inspiration of fresh and splendid endeavour.

This is not that book.

It's merely a book of quotations, inspired by the American humorous writer H. L. Mencken. Looking at William Shakespeare's sundry works, he perceptively argued that all Will did was string together a lot of old, well-known quotations. When I read this it occurred to me that, if heaping together a bunch of old quotes could work for the Bard, well, it might also work for me. I mean, how hard could it be? Harder than I thought, actually. Anyway, this is the result. So a tip of the old quote collector's hat to Mr Mencken for the heads-up on this one!

And speaking of Shakespeare...

I have striven hard to open English eyes to the emptiness of Shakespeare's philosophy, to the superficiality

and second-handedness of his morality, to his weakness
and incoherence as a thinker, to his snobbery, his
vulgar prejudices, his ignorance, his disqualifications
of all sorts for the philosophic eminence claimed
for him...

Who said that? The Irish writer, George Bernard Shaw,
who then added:

With the single exception of Homer, there is no
eminent writer, not even Sir Walter Scott, whom I can
despise so entirely as I despise Shakespeare when I
measure my mind against his ... it would positively be
a relief to me to dig him up and throw stones at him.

I say, GBS, steady on! Shaw v. Shakespeare. Sounds
like the makings of a good old literary feud – if it
wasn't for the fact that Shaw and Shakespeare were
born 292 years apart, making any feud worthy of the
name chronologically impractical.

A better bet was Lord Byron. His contemporaries queued up to feud with him. Why was he, a poet
and leading figure in the Romantic period, so widely
detested? I had no idea of the low regard in which
he was held until I started compiling this book. Lady
Caroline Lamb called him 'mad, bad and dangerous
to know', but she was his sweetheart at the time,
so it sounds more like a boast to her girlfriends,
accompanied by a knowing wink. She didn't exactly
add 'If yah know what ah'm sayin'', but that was her
obvious drift.

George Eliot called Byron a 'vulgar-minded genius', and the Duke of Wellington said of his coterie, 'I hate the whole race of them, there never existed a more worthless set than Byron and his friends.' And even in death he was not free of disapproval. The artist John Constable, on hearing of Byron's death in 1824, reflected, 'The world is rid of Lord Byron, but the deadly slime of his touch still remains.' (Only speak good of the dead. He's dead? Good!)

One of the most poisonous literary feuds of recent years was the one between the two American political firebrands Gore Vidal and Truman Capote. This was Vidal on Capote:

> He's a full-fledged housewife from Kansas with all the prejudices.

And this was Capote on Vidal:

> I guess Gore left the country because he felt that he was underappreciated here. I have news for him: people who actually read his books will under-appreciate him everywhere.

Vidal again:

> It is inhuman to attack Capote. You are attacking an elf.

And again, this time on Capote's death:

> It was a good career move.

The massive growth of social media has led to the democratisation of literary feuding. It's never been easier to fire up a good feud. But who to target? Well, you could start with steering well clear of that elite team of literary notables at Biteback Publishing. To name but seven: Iain Dale, Sam Carter, Lewis Carpenter, Hollie Teague, Namkwan Cho, Olivia Beattie and Charlotte Seymour. Frankly, let me advise you not to mess with any of them. I speak from bitter personal experience!

And what to say? Try borrowing from this book. There are plenty of tart, barbed, cutting and caustic comments lurking within these pages. Many of them eminently tweetable. It's over to you, fellow feuders!

A

#ACKNOWLEDGEMENTS AND DEDICATIONS

To the reader of this book, without whom there would
be no point in being the writer of this book.
  Fred Metcalf, *The Biteback Dictionary of Humorous*
  Literary Quotations (2013)

... a catalogue of favourite aunts, perfect spouses and
the profoundest platitudes. Dedications really do bring
out the worst in authors.
  The Bloomsbury Dictionary of Dedications, ed. by
  Adrian Room (1990)

For my mum, the most important woman in my life,
this book is dedicated to you. Now for God's sake
don't read it.
  Russell Brand, *My Booky Wook: A Memoir of Sex,*
  Drugs and Stand-Up (2007)

Many people, other than the authors, contribute
to the making of a book, from the first person who
had the bright idea of alphabetic writing through the

inventor of movable type to the lumberjacks who felled the trees that were pulped for its printing. It is not customary to acknowledge the trees themselves, though their commitment is total.

  Richard Forsyth and Roy Rada, *Machine Learning*
  (1986)

As an actor and writer Stephen Fry has bestridden the world for a quarter of a century, sowing discord, agitation and dismay. His power grows daily and his disciples are many. However, it is written that at the Time of Leavening, a Chosen One will arise to destroy him. Until that time, Mr Fry will continue to direct, broadcast, act and write in North London and Norfolk, where his best friends are the flowers.

  Stephen Fry, *Making History* (1996)

Neil Gaiman is a messy-haired white male author trapped in the body of an identical white male author with perhaps even less-tidy hair. His books and comics have won many awards. He thanks you for your offer of a comb but does not believe it would do any good. Despite being English, he lives more in America than he does anywhere else in the world, and is currently somewhere in his mid-forties. He wrote this book especially for you.

  Neil Gaiman, *American Gods* (2001)

You know how it is. You pick up a book, flip to the dedication, and find that, once again, the author has dedicated a book to someone else and not you.

Not this time.

Because we haven't yet met/have only a glancing acquaintance/are just crazy about each other/haven't seen each other in much too long/are in some way related/will never meet, but will, I trust, despite that, always think fondly of each other...

This one's for you.

With you know what, and you probably know why.

Neil Gaiman, *Anansi Boys* (2005)

To mankind.

King C. Gillette, *The People's Corporation* (1924)

My dear Lucy, I wrote this story for you, but when I began it I had not realised that girls grow quicker than books. As a result you are already too old for fairy tales, and by the time it is printed and bound you will be older still. But some day you will be old enough to start reading fairy tales again. You can then take it down from some upper shelf, dust it, and tell me what you think of it. I shall probably be too deaf to hear, and too old to understand a word you say, but I shall still be your affectionate Godfather.

C. S. Lewis, *The Lion, the Witch and the Wardrobe* (1950). Dedicated to his god-daughter, Lucy Barfield.

This book is dedicated to my brilliant and beautiful wife without whom I would be nothing. She always comforts and consoles, never complains or interferes, asks nothing, and endures all. She also writes my dedications.
  Albert Malvino, American scientist

This book is dedicated to my bank balance.
  Spike Milligan, *Silly Verse for Kids* (1959)

To my dear brother Desmond, who made my boyhood happy and with whom I have never had a cross word, mind you he drives his wife mad.
  Spike Milligan, *'Rommel?' 'Gunner Who?'* (1974)

To her – Hand in hand we come. Christopher Robin and I. To lay this book in your lap. Say you're surprised? Say you like it? Say it's just what you wanted? Because it's yours – because we love you.
  A. A. Milne, *Winnie-the-Pooh* (1926). Dedicated to his wife.

I hope you get as much pleasure reading my book as I got spending the money you paid me for it.
  Dan Poynter, American writer, publisher and speaker

This book was written using 100% recycled words.
  Terry Pratchett, *Wyrd Sisters* (1988)

This book is dedicated to all the donkeys and mules in the world...

Dr Elisabeth D. Svendsen, *A Passion for Donkeys* (1988)

This book is dedicated to the one woman Fate has created for me. So far I've managed to avoid her.

Jon Winokur, American writer and editor

To my daughter Leonora without whose never-failing sympathy and encouragement this book would have been finished in half the time.

P. G. Wodehouse, *The Heart of a Goof* (1926)

#AGENTS

Talking of agents, when I opened the morning paper one morning last week, I saw that it had finally happened; somebody had shot one. It was probably for the wrong reasons, but at least it was a step in the right direction.

Raymond Chandler, American novelist and screen-writer, letter, 1951

The author's agent fosters in authors the greed for an immediate money return ... at the cost of all dignity and repose.

William Heinemann, English publisher

See also #PUBLISHERS

#AMATEURS AND BEGINNERS

The artistic temperament is a disease that afflicts amateurs.
   G. K. Chesterton, *Heretics* (1905)

There are too many people around who mistake a love of reading with a talent for writing.
   Stanley Ellin, American mystery writer

The first thing a writer has to do is find another source of income.
   Ellen Gilchrist, American novelist and poet

Genius can write on the back of old envelopes but mere talent requires the finest stationery available.
   Dorothy Parker, American wit (attrib.)

A writer who waits for ideal conditions under which to work will die without putting a word on paper.
   E. B. White, interview in the *Paris Review*, autumn 1969

#ARTIST'S LIFE, THE

The artist's wife will know that there is no more sombre enemy of good art than the pram in the hall.
   Cyril Connolly, *Enemies of Promise* (1938)

She is like most artists; she has style without any sincerity.

> Oscar Wilde, 'The Nightingale and the Rose', *The Happy Prince and Other Tales* (1888)

All art is quite useless.

> Oscar Wilde, *The Picture of Dorian Gray* (1890)

No great artist ever sees things as they really are. If he did he would cease to be an artist.

> Oscar Wilde, 'The Decay of Lying' (1891)

A true artist takes no notice whatever of the public. The public to him are non-existent. He leaves that to the popular novelist.

> Oscar Wilde, 'The Soul of Man under Socialism' (1891)

I had a private income – the young artist's best friend.

> P. G. Wodehouse, *Quick Service* (1940)

See also #WRITER'S LIFE, THE

#AUSTEN, JANE
1775–1817, English novelist

Indulge your imagination in every possible flight.

> Jane Austen, *Pride and Prejudice* (1813)

Dear Diary, Today I tried not to think about Mr Knightly. I tried not to think about him when I discussed the menu with Cook ... I tried not to think about him in the garden where I thrice plucked the petals off a daisy to ascertain his feelings for Harriet. I don't think we should keep daisies in the garden, they really are a drab little flower. And I tried not to think about him when I went to bed, but something had to be done.

Jane Austen, *Emma* (1815)

The person, be it gentleman or lady, who has not pleasure in a good novel, must be intolerably stupid.

Jane Austen, *Northanger Abbey* (1817)

... but for my own part, if a book is well written, I always find it too short.

Jane Austen, *Northanger Abbey* (1817)

I do not want people to be very agreeable, as it saves me the trouble of liking them a great deal.

Jane Austen, *Jane Austen's Letters* (1884), ed. by Edward, Lord Brabourne

I think I may boast myself to be, with all possible vanity, the most unlearned and uninformed female who ever dared to be an authoress.

Jane Austen, *Jane Austen's Letters* (1884)

Why do you like Miss Austen so very much? I am puzzled on that point. What induced you to say that you would rather have written *Pride and Prejudice* ... than any of the Waverly novels? I should hardly like to live with her ladies and gentlemen, in their elegant but confined houses.

Charlotte Brontë, English novelist

If there is a heaven, Jane Austen is sitting in a small room with Mother Teresa and Princess Diana, listening to Duran Duran, forever. If there's a hell, she's standing.

Roddy Doyle, Irish novelist and screenwriter

Miss Austen's novels ... seem to me vulgar in tone, sterile in artistic invention, imprisoned in the wretched conventions of English society, without genius, wit, or knowledge of the world. Never was life so pinched and narrow. The one problem in the mind of the writer ... is marriageableness.

Ralph Waldo Emerson, American essayist and poet

I am a Jane Austenite, and therefore slightly imbecile about Jane Austen. My fatuous expression, and airs of personal immunity – how ill they sit on the face, say, of a Stevensonian! But Jane Austen is so different. She is my favourite author! I read and reread, the mouth open and the mind closed. Shut up in measureless content, I greet her by the name of most kind hostess, while criticism slumbers.

E. M. Forster, English novelist

I have discovered that our great favourite, Miss Austen, is my countrywoman ... with whom mamma before her marriage was acquainted. Mamma says that she was then the prettiest, silliest, most affected husband-hunting butterfly she ever remembers.
  Mary Russell Mitford, letter to Sir William Elford, 1815

Jane Austen's novels, which strangely retain their hold on the public taste, are tedious to those who dare to think for themselves.
  Kate Sanborn, American author and teacher

How I wish I lived in a Jane Austen novel!
  Dodie Smith, *I Capture the Castle* (1948)

I haven't any right to criticize books, and I don't do it except when I hate them. I often want to criticize Jane Austen, but her books madden me so that I can't conceal my frenzy from the reader; and therefore I have to stop every time I begin. Every time I read *Pride and Prejudice* I want to dig her up and beat her over the skull with her own shin-bone.
  Mark Twain, American author and humorist

Just the omission of Jane Austen's books alone would make a fairly good library out of a library that hadn't a book in it.
  Mark Twain

#AUSTRALIA

In America, only the successful writer is important, in France all writers are important, in England no writer is important, and in Australia you have to explain what a writer is.

Geoffrey Cotterell, English novelist and wit

In the world of success and failure,
Have you noticed the genius spark
Seems brightest in folk from Australia?
We all leave an indelible mark.
You just have to go to the opera,
Or an art-show, or glance at your shelves
To see in a trice that Australians
Have done *terribly* well for themselves.

Dame Edna Everage (Barry Humphries), 'Terribly Well' (song, 1976)

He plunged into the --- creek,
The --- horse was --- weak,
The --- stockman's face was a --- study!
And though the --- horse was drowned
The --- rider reached the ground
Ejaculating: ---!
---!

W. T. Goodge, 'The Great Australian Adjective', *The Bulletin*

Koala Triangle: a mysterious zone in the Southern Hemisphere where persons of talent disappear without trace.
    Barry Humphries, glossary from *A Nice Night's Entertainment* (1981)

#AUTOBIOGRAPHY

Autobiography is now as common as adultery – and hardly less reprehensible.
    Lord Altrincham, English aristocrat

My brother has just written his memoirs. Memoirs, me arse! You could write that fellow's memoirs on the back of a stamp and still have enough room left for the Koran.
    Brendan Behan, Irish novelist and playwright

Just as there is nothing between the admirable omelette and the intolerable, so with autobiography.
    Hilaire Belloc, English writer

This is the sixth book I've written, which isn't bad for a guy who's only read two.
    George Burns, American nonagenarian comedian

Interest in autobiography should begin at home ... my chief interest is to delight and engross myself. A modest or inhibited autobiography is written without entertainment to the writer and read with distrust by the reader.

Neville Cardus, introduction to *Autobiography* (1947)

An autobiography is an obituary in serial form with the last instalment missing.

Quentin Crisp, *The Naked Civil Servant* (1968)

Democratic societies are unfit for the publication of such thunderous revelations as I am in the habit of making.

Salvador Dalí, Spanish surrealist artist

I'm not saying he's stupid, but his autobiography *won't* be called: *The Man Who Knew Too Much*.

Jerry Dennis, English comedian

My Turn is the distilled bathwater of Mrs Reagan's life. It is for the most part sweetish, with a tart edge of rebuke, but disappointingly free of dirt or particulate matter of any kind.

Barbara Ehrenreich, American feminist and journalist

No one should write their autobiography until after they're dead.

Samuel Goldwyn, American film mogul

Autobiography is an unrivalled vehicle for telling the truth about other people.

Philip Guedalla, British historian and biographer

I am being frank about myself in this book. I tell of my first mistake on page 850.

    Henry Kissinger, on his memoirs *The White House Years*, 1979

The trouble with writing a book about yourself is that you can't fool around. If you write about someone else, you can stretch the truth from here to Finland. If you write about yourself the slightest deviation makes you realize instantly that there may be honor among thieves, but you are just a dirty liar.

    Groucho Marx, American actor and comedian

I read half of my autobiography, then I skipped through. I know what it's about though.

    Dominique Morisseau, American actress, playwright and poet

Autobiography is only to be trusted when it reveals something disgraceful. A man who gives a good account of himself is probably lying, since any life when viewed from the inside is simply a series of defeats.

    George Orwell, English writer and commentator

All those writers who write about their childhood! Gentle God, if I wrote about mine you wouldn't sit in the same room with me.

    Dorothy Parker, American wit

I hear my autobiography is a terrific book. One of these days I may even read it myself.
   Ronald Reagan, US President 1981–9

When you put down the good things you ought to have done, and leave out the bad things you did do – that's Memoirs.
   Will Rogers, American humorist

I have decided to keep a full journal, in the hope that my life will perhaps seem more interesting when it is written down.
   Sue Townsend, *Adrian Mole: The Wilderness Years* (1993)

Don't give your opinions about Art and the Purpose of Life. They are of little interest and, anyway, you can't express them. Don't analyse yourself. Give the relevant facts and let your readers make their own judgments. Stick to your story. It is not the most important subject in history but it is one about which you are uniquely qualified to speak.
   Evelyn Waugh, English novelist

Only when one has lost all curiosity about the future has one reached the age to write an autobiography.
   Evelyn Waugh

Hiring someone to write your autobiography is like paying someone to take a bath for you.
   Mae West, American actress

I dislike modern memoirs. They are generally written by people who have either entirely lost their memories, or have never done anything worth remembering.
    Oscar Wilde, Irish writer, essayist and playwright

I'm writing an unauthorized autobiography.
    Steven Wright, American comedian

See also #BIOGRAPHY, #DIARIES

#AWARDS

I don't deserve this, but then, I have arthritis and I don't deserve that either.
    Jack Benny, American comedian, on accepting an award

The book trade invented literary prizes to stimulate sales, not to reward merit.
    Michael Moorcock, English science fiction writer

Nobel Prize money is a lifebelt thrown to a swimmer who has already reached the shore in safety.
    George Bernard Shaw, Irish playwright

To refuse awards is another way of accepting them with more noise than is normal.
    Mark Twain, American author and humorist

B

#BESTSELLERS

Despite being a bestseller in the United States, *The Corrections* is really a wonderful novel.
   Ramona Koval, Australian writer and broadcaster

I am the kind of writer that people think other people are reading.
   V. S. Naipaul, Trinidadian–British novelist

The principle of procrastinated rape is said to be the ruling one in all the great bestsellers.
   V. S. Pritchett, English writer

See also #BOOKS, #SUCCESS

#BIBLE, THE

The first pair ate the first apple.
   Anon.

Scriptures, n., The sacred books of our holy religion, as distinguished from the false and profane writings on which all other faiths are based.

    Ambrose Bierce, *The Devil's Dictionary* (1911)

I had occasion to read the Bible the other night and believe me it is a lesson in how not to write for the movies. The worst kind of overwriting. Whole chapters that could have been said in one paragraph. And the dialogue!

    Raymond Chandler, American novelist and
    screenwriter

And Noah he often said to his wife when he sat down to dine,
'I don't care where the water goes if it doesn't get into the wine.'

    G. K. Chesterton, 'Wine and Water', *The Flying Inn*
    (1914)

It is not fair to visit all
The blame on Eve, for Adam's fall;
The most Eve did was to display
Contributory negligee.

    Oliver Herford, 'Eve: Apropos de Rien'

If it was the exact word of God, it would be real clear and easy to understand. God's got a way with words, being the creator of language and all.

    Bill Hicks, American comedian

The inspiration of the Bible depends upon the ignorance of the gentleman who reads it.

Robert G. Ingersoll, American political leader, nicknamed 'The Great Agnostic'

I want to read the employment section of the Bible. I think it's simply called Job.

Jarod Kintz, American novelist

The Bible contains six admonishments to homosexuals and 362 to heterosexuals. That doesn't mean that God doesn't like heterosexuals, just that they need more supervision.

Lynn Lavner, American comedian

From 'Top ten words used least in the Bible'
– Perky
– Fudge-a-licious
– Rootin'-tootin'
– Schweppervescence
– Gas-guzzling

David Letterman, *The Late Show*, CBS

Like many classics, the New Testament is not very well written.

Norman Mailer, American writer and film-maker

Say what you will about the Ten Commandments, you always come back to the pleasant fact that there are only ten of them.

H. L. Mencken, American humorist

The Good Book – one of the most remarkable euphe-
misms ever coined.

> Ashley Montagu, British–American humanist and
> anthropologist

It is a curious thing that God learned Greek when
he wished to turn author – and that he did not learn
it better.

> Friedrich Nietzsche, German critic, philosopher and
> philologist

The Bible has noble poetry in it … and some good
morals and a wealth of obscenity, and upwards of a
thousand lies.

> Mark Twain, American author and humorist

It ain't those parts of the Bible that I can't understand
that bother me, it is the parts I do understand.

> Mark Twain

Even if you don't believe a word of the Bible, you've
got to respect the person who typed all that.

> Lotus Weinstock, American comedian

The total absence of humour from the Bible is one of
the most singular things in all literature.

> Alfred North Whitehead, English mathematician and
> philosopher

I think God, in creating man, somewhat overestimated his ability.

Oscar Wilde, Irish writer, essayist and playwright

#BIOGRAPHY

A well-written Life is almost as rare as a well-spent one.

Thomas Carlyle, Scottish philosopher, essayist and historian

Biographies are likely either to be acts of worship or acts of destruction. And the best ones have elements of both.

Humphrey Carpenter, English biographer, writer and broadcaster, 1995

Reformers are always finally neglected, while the memoirs of the frivolous will always be eagerly read.

Henry 'Chips' Channon, cited in R. R. James (ed.), *'Chips': The Diaries of Sir Henry Channon* (1967)

Anyone turning biographer commits himself to lies, to concealment, to hypocrisy, to flattery and even to hiding his own lack of understanding, for biographical truth is not to be had and even if it were, it couldn't be used.

Sigmund Freud, Austrian psychoanalyst, to a writer who had suggested being his biographer

Biographers know nothing about the intimate sex lives of their own wives but they think they know all about Stendahl's or Faulkner's.

Milan Kundera, Franco-Czech novelist, 1995

Biography is in some ways the most brutish of all the arts. It shifts about uncomfortably in the strangely uncertain middle ground between deliberate assassination and helpless boot-licking.

Dennis Potter, English screenwriter and journalist, 1968

I never read the life of an important person without discovering that he knew more and could do more than I could ever hope to know or to do in half a dozen lifetimes.

J. B. Priestley, English novelist, playwright and broadcaster

When you put down the good things you ought to have done, and leave out the bad things you did do, that's memoirs.

Will Rogers, American humorist

I hope the next time she crosses a street, four blind guys come along driving cars.

Frank Sinatra, American singer, of his biographer Kitty Kelley

Just how difficult it is to write biography can be reckoned by anybody who sits down and considers just how many people know the real truth about his or her love affairs.
Rebecca West, English author and literary critic

Every great man nowadays has his disciples and it is always Judas who writes the biography.
Oscar Wilde, Irish writer, essayist and playwright, 1891

Biography lends to death a new terror.
Oscar Wilde

See also #AUTOBIOGRAPHY, #DIARIES

#BOOKS

Thank you for sending me a copy of your book. I'll waste no time in reading it.
Anon.

Never lend books, my son. Only fools lend books. Once, all these books belonged to fools!
Anon., cited in F. Dennis, *Tales from the Woods* (2010)

How much sooner one tires of anything than of a book!
Jane Austen, *Pride and Prejudice* (1813)

Provided that nothing like useful knowledge could be gained from them, provided they were all story and no reflection, she had never any objection to books at all.
  Jane Austen, *Northanger Abbey* (1817)

Some books should be tasted, some devoured, but only a few should be chewed and digested thoroughly.
  Sir Francis Bacon, English philosopher, statesman and author

Books will speak plain when counsellors blanch.
  Sir Francis Bacon, 'Of Counsel' (1625)

Books say: She did this because. Life says: She did this. Books are where things are explained to you; life is where things aren't. I'm not surprised some people prefer books.
  Julian Barnes, *Flaubert's Parrot* (1984)

Child! do not throw this book about;
Refrain from the unholy pleasure
Of cutting all the pictures out!
Preserve it as your chiefest treasure.
  Hilaire Belloc, *Bad Child's Book of Beasts* (1896)

DUFF: We've had a big bestseller ... I haven't got round to it yet. I suspect the presence of allegory, which is always a slight deterrent.
  Alan Bennett, *The Old Country* (1978)

I wonder if what we are publishing now is worth cutting down trees to make paper for the stuff.
  Richard Brautigan, American poet

There is a good saying to the effect that when a new book appears one should read an old one. As an author I would not recommend too strict an adherence to this saying.
  Sir Winston Churchill, British Prime Minister
  1940–45, 1951–5

To be a book-collector is to combine the worst characteristics of a dope fiend with those of a miser.
  Robertson Davies, *The Table Talk of Samuel Marchbanks* (1949)

A note to those who bought the book *Skydiving Made Easy*: There is a correction on page 11 paragraph 4. The words 'state zip code' should be changed to 'pull rip cord'.
  Jerry Dennis, English comedian

The love of books is among the choicest gifts of the gods.
  Sir Arthur Conan Doyle, Scottish physician and writer

When I have a little money, I buy books; and if I have any left, I buy food and clothes.
  Erasmus (Desiderius Erasmus Roterodamus), Dutch humanist and theologian

Most new books are forgotten within a year, especially by those who borrow them.
  Evan Esar, American wit

It is a mistake to think that books have come to stay. The human race did without them for thousands of years and may decide to do without them again.
  E. M. Forster, English novelist

Books have to be read (worse luck it takes so long a time). It is the only way of discovering what they contain. A few savage tribes eat them but reading is the only method of assimilation revealed to the West.
  E. M. Forster

Never lend books, for no one ever returns them; the only books I have in my library are books that other folk have lent me.
  Anatole France, French poet, journalist and novelist

The most technologically efficient machine that man has ever invented is the book.
  Northrop Frye, Canadian literary critic and theorist

When I was your age, television was called books.
  William Goldman, *The Princess Bride* (1973)

ERRATUM
This slip has been inserted by mistake.
  Alasdair Gray, erratum slip inserted in *Unlikely Stories, Mostly* (1983)

There is no friend as loyal as a book.
  Ernest Hemingway, American novelist and journalist

Books are the perfect entertainment: no commercials, no batteries, hours of enjoyment for each dollar spent. What I wonder is why everybody doesn't carry a book around for those inevitable dead spots in life.
  Stephen King, American novelist

Good books don't give up all their secrets at once.
  Stephen King

A book reads the better which is your own, and has been so long known to us, that we know the topography of its blots, and dog's ears, and can trace the dirt in it to having read it at tea with buttered muffins.
  Charles Lamb, English essayist

You can never get a cup of tea large enough or a book long enough to suit me.
  C. S. Lewis, English novelist and theologian

Books serve to show a man that those original thoughts of his aren't very new after all.
  Abraham Lincoln, US President 1861–5

Books to the ceiling, Books to the sky,
My pile of books is a mile high.
How I love them! How I need them!
I'll have a long beard by the time I read them.
  Arnold Lobel, American author and illustrator

There is no tribe of human beings more pestiferous than the people who insist on lending you books whether you wish to borrow them or not.
  Robert Lynd, Irish writer and essayist

Lord! when you sell a man a book you don't sell just twelve ounces of paper and ink and glue – you sell him a whole new life. Love and friendship and humour and ships at sea by night – there's all heaven and earth in a book, a real book.
  Christopher Morley, American journalist, poet and
  playwright

Book Given As Gift Actually Read
LONG BEACH, CA – The nation's publishing industry was rocked by Monday's news that a book given as a holiday gift was actually read and enjoyed by its recipient. According to reports, Long Beach schoolteacher Gavin Wallace completed James Gleick's *Genius: The Life and Science of Richard Feynman*, a present from his cousin.

…Wallace previously made headlines for his December 1996 consumption of a Hickory Farms gift basket.
  The Onion, 22 December 1999

Wear the old coat and buy the new book.
  Austin Phelps, American Congregationalist minister
  and educator

My favourite writers are Joyce, Tolstoy, Proust and Flaubert, but right now I am reading *The Little Engine That Could*.
Emo Philips, American comedian

Some men borrow books; some men steal books; and others beg presentation copies from the author.
James Jeffrey Roche, Irish–American poet, journalist and diplomat

I hate books; they only teach us to talk about things we know nothing about.
Jean-Jacques Rousseau, *Emile* (1762)

Books ... are like lobster shells, we surround ourselves with 'em, then we grow out of 'em and leave 'em behind, as evidence of our earlier stages of development.
Dorothy L. Sayers, *The Unpleasantness at the Bellona Club* (1928)

Buying books would be a good thing if one could also find the time to read them; but as a rule the purchase of books is mistaken for the appropriation of their contents.
Arthur Schopenhauer, German philosopher

If a book about failures doesn't sell, is it a success?
Jerry Seinfeld, American comedian

Reading good books ruins you for enjoying bad books.
Mary Ann Shaffer, *The Guernsey Literary and Potato Peel Pie Society* (2008)

No furniture is so charming as books, even if you never open them or read a single word.
   Sydney Smith, English wit and clergyman

Books – the best antidote against the marsh-gas of boredom and vacuity.
   George Steiner, American philosopher and novelist

Books are good enough in their own way but they are a mighty bloodless substitute for life.
   Robert Louis Stevenson, 'An Apology for Idlers',
   Virginibus Puerisque (1881)

Good friends, good books and a sleepy conscience: this is the ideal life.
   Mark Twain, American author and humorist

I like a thin book because it will steady a table; a leather volume because it will strop a razor; and a heavy book because it can be thrown at the cat.
   Mark Twain

Books are for people who wish they were somewhere else.
   Mark Twain

Be careful about reading health books. You may die of a misprint.
   Mark Twain

Date a girl who reads. Date a girl who spends her money on books instead of clothes, who has problems with closet space because she has too many books. Date a girl who has a list of books she wants to read, who has had a library card since she was twelve.

Rosemarie Urquico, Filipino writer

If you go home with somebody, and they don't have books, don't fuck 'em!

John Waters, American screenwriter and film director

They borrow books they will not buy,
They have no ethics or religions;
I wish some kind Burbankian guy
Could cross my books with homing pigeons.

Carolyn Wells, 'Book-borrowers'

Masterpieces is a bouquet of *pensées*, culled, garnered and even untimely ripped from the fertile loins of the Wellsian imagination, time-weatherered flotsam plucked from the raging delirium tremens of the creative process.

Here are jewelled insights, lovingly crafted by a veritable Fabergé amongst wordsmiths, hand-polished erections in the global village of contemporary sensibility, perceptions snatched from the outer limits of human experience, great miniatures acid-etched on the tender *film noir* of the mind's membrane ... *Masterpieces* ... The paperback!

John Wells, *Masterpieces* (1982)

Anthologies are just pre-digested food for the brain.
Rebecca West, English author and literary critic

If one cannot enjoy reading a book over and over again, there is no use in reading it at all.
Oscar Wilde, Irish writer, essayist and playwright

Books had instant replay long before televised sports.
Bern Williams, American author

A magnum opus is a book which, when dropped from a three-storey building, is big enough to kill a man.
Edward Wilson, English novelist

Book collecting is an obsession, an occupation, a disease, an addiction, a fascination, an absurdity, a fate. It is not a hobby. Those who do it must do it. Those who do not do it, think of it as a cousin of stamp collecting, a sister of the trophy cabinet, bastard of a sound bank account and a weak mind.
Jeanette Winterson, English novelist

I have hundreds of books, but no bookcase. Nobody would lend me a bookcase.
Henny Youngman, British–American comedian

I think it is good that books still exist, but they do make me sleepy.
Frank Zappa, American singer-songwriter

So many books, so little time.
  Frank Zappa

See also #BESTSELLERS, #BOOKSHOPS, #NOVELS

#BOOKSHOPS

Where is human nature so weak as in the bookstore?
  Henry Ward Beecher, American clergyman and social
  reformer

I went to a bookstore and asked the saleswoman,
'Where's the self-help section?' She said if she told me,
it would defeat the purpose.
  George Carlin, American comedian

I did discover that if you're interested in low wages, a
bookstore ranks below retail clothing sales, except the
hours are worse.
  Sue Grafton, American mystery writer

A literary academic can no more pass a bookstore
than an alcoholic can pass a bar.
  Carolyn G. Heilbrun, American feminist author

If you want to know who the oppressed minorities in
America are, simply look at who gets their own shelf
in the bookstore. A black shelf, a women's shelf, and
a gay shelf.
  Armistead Maupin, American writer

Aziraphale collected books. If he were totally honest with himself he would have to have admitted that his bookshop was simply somewhere to store them. He was not unusual in this. In order to maintain his cover as a typical second-hand book seller, he used every means short of actual physical violence to prevent customers from making a purchase. Unpleasant damp smells, glowering looks, erratic opening hours – he was incredibly good at it.

Terry Pratchett and Neil Gaiman, *Good Omens: The Nice and Accurate Prophecies of Agnes Nutter, Witch* (1990)

The smallest bookstore still contains more ideas of worth than have been presented in the entire history of television.

Andrew Ross, American author, editor and cultural analyst

#BYRON, LORD
1788–1824, English Romantic poet

Byron! – he would be all forgotten today if he had lived to be a florid old gentleman with iron-grey whiskers, writing very long, very able letters to *The Times* about the repeal of the Corn Laws.

Max Beerbohm, English writer and critic

The world is rid of Lord Byron, but the deadly slime of his touch still remains.

   John Constable, English painter, on hearing of Lord
   Byron's death, 1824

He seems to me the most vulgar-minded genius that ever produced a great effect in literature.

   George Eliot, English novelist

... mad, bad and dangerous to know.

   Lady Caroline Lamb, British aristocrat and novelist,
   1812

Byron can only bore the spleen.

   Charles Lamb, English essayist

I never heard a single expression of fondness for him fall from the lips of those who knew him well.

   Thomas Babington Macaulay, English historian and
   politician

... always looking at himself in mirrors to make sure he was sufficiently outrageous.

   Enoch Powell, British Conservative politician

I hate the whole race of them, there never existed a more worthless set than Byron and his friends.

   Arthur Wellesley, Duke of Wellington, British soldier
   and statesman

C

#CENSORSHIP

A censor believes in life, liberty and the pursuit of other people's happiness.
> Anon.

There's so much comedy on television. Does that cause comedy in the streets?
> Dick Cavett, American television talk show host, 1994

If we don't believe in freedom of expression for people we despise, we don't believe in it at all.
> Noam Chomsky, American philosopher, critic and activist

Censorship is when we stop people reading or seeing what we do not want to read or see ourselves.
> Lord Diplock, English judge and law lord

If all printers were determined not to print anything till they were sure it would offend nobody, there would be very little printed.

Benjamin Franklin, American Founding Father

History proves there is no better advertisement for a book than to condemn it for obscenity.

Holbrook Jackson, English writer, journalist and publisher

Did you ever hear anyone say, 'That work had better be banned because I might read it and it might be very damaging to me'?

Joseph Henry Jackson, American Baptist pastor

Censorship, like charity, should begin at home; but, unlike charity, it should end there.

Clare Boothe Luce, American writer and diplomat

Censorship of anything, at any time, in any place, on whatever pretense, has always been and always will be the last resort of the boob and the bigot.

Eugene O'Neill, American playwright

A censor is a man who knows more than he thinks you ought to.

Dr Laurence J. Peter, *Peter's Quotations* (1977)

Censorship ends in logical completeness when nobody is allowed to read any books except the books that nobody reads.

George Bernard Shaw, Irish playwright

If a man is pictured chopping off a woman's breast, it only gets an 'R' rating; but if, God forbid, a man is pictured kissing a woman's breast, it gets an 'X' rating. Why is violence more acceptable than tenderness?
  Sally Struthers, quoted in *Life* magazine, 1984

Censorship is telling a man he can't have a steak just because a baby can't chew it.
  Mark Twain, American author and humorist

Nature knows no indecencies; man invents them.
  Mark Twain, *Notebook* (1935), ed. by Albert Bigelow Paine

The English public takes no interest in a work of art until it is told that the work in question is immoral.
  Oscar Wilde, Irish writer, essayist and playwright

The dirtiest book of all is the expurgated book.
  Walt Whitman, American writer

If you are a songwriter, did anyone ask you if you wanted to spend the rest of your career modifying your lyric content to suit the spiritual needs of an imaginary eleven-year-old?
  Frank Zappa, *The Real Frank Zappa Book* (1990)

See also #PORNOGRAPHY

#CHARACTER

I'm not too keen on characters taking over; they do as they are damn well told.
Iain Banks, Scottish novelist, 1993

I sometimes lose interest in the characters and get much more interested in the trees and animals.
Toni Morrison, American novelist, editor and professor, 1989

They require that the author shall make the reader feel a deep interest in the personages of his tale and in their fate; and that he shall make the reader love the good people in the tale and hate the bad ones. But the reader of the *Deerslayer* tale dislikes the good people in it, is indifferent to the others, and wishes they would all get drowned together.
Mark Twain, detailing eighteen rules of fiction, reviewing *The Deerslayer* by James Fenimore Cooper

#CHEKHOV, ANTON
1860–1904, Russian physician, playwright and author

Medicine is my lawful wife and literature is my mistress. When I grow tired of one, I spend the night with the other.
Letters of Anton Chekhov, 11 September 1888

Don't tell me the moon is shining; show me the glint of light on broken glass.
    Anton Chekhov (attrib.)

#CHILDREN'S BOOKS

Children's Books You *Won't* See:
• Garfield Gets Feline Leukemia
• You Are Different and That's Bad
• Daddy Drinks Because You Cry
• Strangers Have the Best Candy
• Why Can't Mr Fork and Miss Electrical Outlet Be Friends?
• The Kid's Guide to Hitchhiking
• What Is That Dog Doing to That Other Dog?
• The Boy Who Died Through Eating All His Vegetables
• Controlling the Playground – Respect Through Fear
    Anon.

Victorian children's stories are full of children who cannot read anywhere except in a deeply embrasured window seat.
    Robertson Davies, Canadian writer and critic, 1990

A children's story that can only be enjoyed by children is not a good children's story in the slightest.
    C. S. Lewis, English novelist and theologian

#CLASSICS, THE

I took a speed-reading course and read *War and Peace* in twenty minutes. It involves Russia.
  Woody Allen, American film-maker and actor

If I had to live my life all over again, there is only one thing I would change. I wouldn't read *Moby Dick*.
  Woody Allen

Definition of a classic: a book everyone is assumed to have read and often think they have.
  Alan Bennett, English diarist and playwright, 1991

The greatest masterpiece in literature is only a dictionary out of order.
  Jean Cocteau, French poet, novelist and dramatist

After I read Kafka at college, I went home for Christmas and suddenly saw my family anew, with complete clarity.
  Jonathan Franzen, American novelist

I like to take a Trollope to bed, but if one is not available, I will settle for a Wodehouse.
  Harold Macmillan, British Prime Minister 1957–63

A man came to my door and said, 'I'd like to read your
gas meter.' I said, 'Whatever happened to the classics?'
   Emo Philips, American comedian

Classic. A book which people praise and don't read.
   Mark Twain, *Following the Equator* (1897)

A classic is something that everyone wants to read.
   Mark Twain, 'The Disappearance of Literature'
   (speech, 1900)

I haven't read Karl Marx. I got stuck on that footnote
on page two.
   Harold Wilson, British Prime Minister 1964–70,
   1974–6

See also #BESTSELLERS, #BOOKS, #GREAT WRITERS

#CLICHÉS

Hush little bright line,
Don't you cry,
You'll be a cliché
By and by.
   Fred Allen, American comedian

What does it behove us to proclaim?

Our faith.

In what does it behove us to proclaim our faith?

Democracy.

From what vertiginous eyrie does it behove us to proclaim our faith in democracy?

From the house-tops.

At what time should we proclaim our faith in democracy from the house-tops?

Now, more than ever.

> Myles na Gopaleen, 'The Myles na Gopaleen
> Catechism of Clichés', *The Best of Myles na
> Gopaleen*, ed. by Flann O'Brien (1968)

#CREATIVITY

Creativity is allowing yourself to make mistakes. Art is knowing which ones to keep.

> Scott Adams, American cartoonist and satirist

Here's my theory about meetings and life: the three things you can't fake are erections, competence and creativity.

> Douglas Coupland, *JPod* (2006)

I make more mistakes than anyone else I know, and sooner or later, I patent most of them.

> Thomas Edison, American inventor and businessman

The secret to creativity is knowing how to hide your sources.
  Albert Einstein, German-born theoretical physicist

Anxiety is the hand maiden of creativity.
  T. S. Eliot, American poet and critic

Anxiety is the essential condition of intellectual and artistic creation ... and everything that is finest in human history.
  Charles Frankel, American philosopher

Creativity is the sudden cessation of stupidity.
  Edwin Land, American scientist and inventor

Doors are for people with no imagination.
  Derek Landy, *Skulduggery Pleasant* (2007)

Creativity is thinking up new things. Innovation is doing new things.
  Theodore Levitt, American professor, economist and editor

Things are only impossible until they're not.
  Jean-Luc Picard, character in *Star Trek*

The urge to destroy is also a creative urge.
  Pablo Picasso, Spanish painter and sculptor

Learn the rules like a pro, so you can break them like an artist.
Pablo Picasso

The chief enemy of creativity is good sense.
Pablo Picasso

Ah, good taste! What a dreadful thing! Taste is the enemy of creativeness.
Pablo Picasso

Every child is an artist. The problem is how to remain an artist once he grows up.
Pablo Picasso

Thank goodness I was never sent to school; it would have rubbed off some of the originality.
Beatrix Potter, English children's author

An idea that is not dangerous is unworthy of being called an idea at all.
Oscar Wilde, Irish writer, essayist and playwright

#CRITICS AND CRITICISM

A thick skin is a gift from God.
Konrad Adenauer, German Chancellor 1949–63

He writes so well, he makes me feel like putting my quill back in my goose.

Fred Allen, American comedian

I was very excited by his last book, mainly because I hoped it was.

Anon.

I got a free copy of this book and I still feel cheated.

Anon.

Writing about art is like dancing about architecture.

Anon.

I am returning this otherwise good typing paper to you because someone has printed gibberish all over it and put your name at the top.

Anonymous professor to anonymous student

One of the first and most important things for a critic to learn is how to sleep undetected at the theatre.

William Archer, Scottish critic

When I dislike what I see on the stage, I can be vastly amusing, but when I write about something I like, I am appallingly dull.

Max Beerbohm, English writer and critic

The covers of this book are too far apart.

Ambrose Bierce, American author and critic

A good writer is not, per se, a good critic. No more than a good drunk is automatically a good bartender.
   Jim Bishop, American journalist and author

That trees should have been cut down to provide paper for this book was an ecological affront.
   Anthony Blond, *The Spectator*, 1983

To many people, dramatic criticism must be like trying to tattoo soap bubbles.
   John Mason Brown, American author and drama
   critic

Either criticism is no good at all (a very defensible position) or else criticism means saying about an author the very things that would have made him jump out of his boots.
   G. K. Chesterton, *Charles Dickens* (1906)

Whom the Gods wish to destroy they first call promising.
   Cyril Connolly, *Enemies of Promise* (1938)

Sartor Resartus is simply unreadable, and for me that always sort of spoils a book.
   Will Cuppy, American humorist and literary critic

One always tends to overpraise a long book because one has got through it.
   E. M. Forster, English novelist

Criticism is a study by which men grow important and formidable at very small expense.

   Samuel Johnson, English poet, biographer and
   lexicographer

One of the greatest creations of the human mind is the art of reviewing books without having to read them.

   G. C. Lichtenberg, German scientist and satirist

People who like this sort of thing will find this the sort of thing they like.

   Abraham Lincoln, US President 1861–5

He writes as though his prose has been fed through Google translate. Twice.

   Alex Massie, Scottish journalist, on the American
   actor and activist Sean Penn, *The Spectator*, 2012

From the moment I picked your book up until I laid it down, I convulsed with laughter. Someday I intend on reading it.

   Groucho Marx, American actor and comedian

I was so long writing my review that I never got round to reading the book.

   Groucho Marx

People ask you for criticism, but they only want praise.

   W. Somerset Maugham, *Of Human Bondage* (1915)

A critic is a person who surprises the playwright by informing him what he meant.

Wilson Mizner, American playwright and raconteur

It is written without fear and without research.

Dorothy Parker, American wit

The love affair between Margot Asquith and Margot Asquith will live as one of the prettiest love stories in all literature.

Dorothy Parker

This is not a novel to be tossed aside lightly. It should be thrown with great force.

Dorothy Parker, in a book review

Q. If you were to be marooned on a desert island and had the whole of Canadian literature to choose from, what would you take?
A. Poison.

Sally Poplin, English writer

There's a certain kind of conversation you have from time to time at parties in New York about a new book. The word 'banal' sometimes rears its by-now banal head; you say 'under-edited', I say 'derivative'. The conversation goes around and around various literary criticisms, and by the time it moves on one thing is clear: No one read the book; we just read the reviews.

Anna Quindlen, American author and columnist

The only reason I didn't kill myself after I read the reviews of my first book was because we have two rivers in New York and I couldn't decide which one to jump into.

Wilfrid Sheed, English-born American novelist and essayist

I never read a book before reviewing it – it prejudices a man so.

Sydney Smith, English wit and clergyman

To see him fumbling with our rich and delicate language is to experience all the horror of seeing a Sèvres vase in the hands of a chimpanzee.

Evelyn Waugh, reviewing *World Within World* by Steven Spender, 1951

He leads his readers to the latrine and locks them in.

Oscar Wilde, Irish writer, essayist and playwright, on the novelist and playwright George Moore

George Meredith. His style is chaos illuminated by flashes of lightning. As a writer he has mastered everything except language: as a novelist he can do everything except tell a story: as an artist he is everything except articulate.

Oscar Wilde, 'The Decay of Lying' (1891)

Mr Hall Caine, it is true, aims at the grandiose, but then he writes at the top of his voice. He is so loud that one cannot hear what he says.

Oscar Wilde, 'The Decay of Lying' (1891)

M. Zola is determined to show that, if he has not got genius, he can at least be dull.

Oscar Wilde, 'The Decay of Lying' (1891)

I could see by the way she sniffed that she was about to become critical. There had always been a strong strain of book-reviewer blood in her.

P. G. Wodehouse, *Aunts Aren't Gentlemen* (1974)

See also #CRITICS – REVIEWS, #WRITERS VERSUS CRITICS

#CRITICS – REVIEWS

If I were ever going to read a book, it would be this one.

Caroline Aherne, English actress and comedian, cover quote for *My Canapé Hell* by Imogen Edwards-Jones, 2000

A man standing up to his neck in a cesspool and adding to its contents.

Anon., on Algernon Swinburne, English poet and critic

I don't think Robert Browning was very good in bed. His wife probably didn't care for him very much. He snored and had fantasies about twelve-year-old girls.

> W. H. Auden, Anglo-American poet, on the English
> poet and playwright

The Far Pavilions is one of those big, fat paperbacks intended to while away a monsoon or two, which, if thrown with a good overarm action, will bring a water buffalo to its knees.

> Nancy Banks-Smith, English journalist and critic

Are we in the West so shaken in our sense of ourselves and our culture, are we so disablingly terrified in the face of the various fanaticisms which threaten us, that we can allow ourselves to be persuaded and comforted by such a self-satisfied and, in many ways, ridiculous novel as this?

> John Banville, English novelist, *New York Review of
> Books*, reviewing Ian McEwan's *Saturday*, 2009

I would rather read a novel about civil servants written by a rabbit.

> Craig Brown, English humorist and critic, on
> *Watership Down* by Richard Adams

… we have made efforts almost as superhuman as the story itself appears to be, to get through it; but with the fullest stretch of our perseverance, we are forced to confess that we have not been able to struggle beyond the first of the four books…

[Mr Keats] is a copyist ... but he is more unintelligible, almost as rugged, twice as diffuse, and ten times more tiresome and absurd than his prototype, who, though he impudently presumed to seat himself in the chair of criticism, and to measure his own poetry by his own standard, yet generally had a meaning.

John Wilson Croker, Irish statesman and author,
reviewing *Endymion* by John Keats, 1818

When it comes down to it, *Lucky Jim* is *Just William*, bigger and bespectacled, literate and funny, but scarcely grown-up.

Simon Gray, English playwright, on *Lucky Jim* by
Kingsley Amis, English author

Vidal's phrasings sometimes used to have a certain rotundity and extravagance, but now he has descended straight to the cheap, and even to the counterfeit. What business does this patrician have in the gutter markets, where paranoids jabber and the coinage is debased by every sort of vulgarity?

Christopher Hitchens, in *Vanity Fair*, on American
critic and commentator Gore Vidal, 2010

Nature, not content with denying him the ability to think, has endowed him with the ability to write.

A. E. Housman, English Classical scholar and poet

It has taken thirty-three years for Jean-Paul Sartre's *The Devil and the Good Lord* to reach London, but our luck was bound to run out sooner or later.

    Kenneth Hurren, English theatre critic, *Mail on Sunday*

It is utterly incompetent to the primary functions of a book...

We do not open his books with the expectation of being thrilled, or convinced, or deeply moved in any way, and, accordingly, when we find one to be as flat as a Dutch landscape, we remind ourselves that we have wittingly travelled into Holland, and that we have no right to abuse the scenery for being in character.

Our great objection to *The Belton Estate* is that, as we read it, we seemed to be reading a work written for children; a work prepared for minds unable to think; a work below the apprehension of the average man and woman...

    Henry James, American novelist, reviewing *The Belton Estate* by Anthony Trollope, 1866

Have you ever struggled through one of Salman Rushdie's books to the end? Neither have I and neither, I bet, did the Ayatollah.

    Boris Johnson, Mayor of London

Your manuscript is both good and original, but the part that is good is not original and the part that is original is not good.

    Samuel Johnson, English poet, biographer and lexicographer

Paradise Lost is one of those books which the reader admires, lays down and forgets to take up again. Never ever wished it longer than it is.

Samuel Johnson, on John Milton's epic poem

A play in which nothing happens, twice.

Vivian Mercier, *Irish Times*, on *Waiting for Godot* by Samuel Beckett, 1954

A work of art? It has no invention; it has no order, system, sequence, or result; it has no lifelikeness, no thrill, no stir, no seeming of reality; its characters are confusedly drawn, and by their acts and words they prove that they are not the sort of people the author claims that they are; its humor is pathetic; its pathos is funny; its conversations are – oh! indescribable; its love-scenes odious; its English a crime against the language.

Mark Twain, reviewing *The Deerslayer* by James Fenimore Cooper

Cooper's art has some defects. In one place in *Deerslayer*, and in the restricted space of two-thirds of a page, Cooper has scored 114 offences against literary art out of a possible 115. It breaks the record.

Mark Twain, reviewing *The Deerslayer* by James Fenimore Cooper

[Ambrose] Bierce has written some admirable things
– fugitive pieces – but none of them are 'Nuggets'.
There is humor in Dod Grile, but for every laugh that
is in his book there are five blushes, ten shudders & a
vomit. The laugh is too expensive.
  Mark Twain, letter to Chatto & Windus, 8 April 1874

… in a long career he appears to have known practically no one … Perhaps Powell should have stayed
in the Intelligence Corps officers' mess. That, I feel, is
where his heart belongs.
  Auberon Waugh, *Daily Telegraph*, reviewing a collec-
  tion of work by Anthony Powell, 1990

I always review my friends' books, it's so much less
trouble than reading them.
  Evelyn Waugh, English novelist

Its central character, Alex-Li Tandem, is a dreary
blank, an empty centre entirely filled by his pop-
culture devotions. Around him swirls a text incapable
of ever stiffening into sobriety, a flailing, noisy hash of
jokes, cool cultural references, pull-quotes, lists and
roaring italics. It is like reading a newspaper designed
by a kindergarten.
  James Wood, *London Review of Books*, reviewing
  The Autograph Man by Zadie Smith, 2002

See also #CRITICS AND CRITICISM, #WRITERS
VERSUS CRITICS

#CULTURE

One of the basic freedoms of the Englishman is freedom from culture.
Lord Goodman, Chairman of the Arts Council, 1967

Culture is roughly anything we do and the monkeys don't.
Lord Raglan, British soldier

Mrs Ballinger is one of the ladies who pursue Culture in bands, as though it were dangerous to meet it alone.
Edith Wharton, *Xingu* (1916)

D

#DEATH

See #LAST WORDS, #OBITUARIES

#DIALOGUE

They require that when the personages of a tale deal in conversation, the talk shall sound like human talk, and be talk such as human beings would be likely to talk in the given circumstances, and have a discoverable meaning, also a discoverable purpose, and a show of relevancy, and remain in the neighborhood of the subject at hand, and be interesting to the reader, and help out the tale, and stop when the people cannot think of anything more to say. But this requirement has been ignored from the beginning of the *Deerslayer* tale to the end of it.

Mark Twain, detailing eighteen rules of fiction,
reviewing *The Deerslayer* by James Fenimore Cooper

They require that when a personage talks like an illustrated, gilt-edged, tree-calf, hand-tooled, seven-dollar Friendship's Offering in the beginning of a paragraph, he shall not talk like a negro minstrel in the end of it. But this rule is flung down and danced upon in the *Deerslayer* tale.

> Mark Twain, detailing eighteen rules of fiction, reviewing *The Deerslayer* by James Fenimore Cooper

#DIARIES

It's the good girls who keep the diaries. The bad girls never have the time.

> Tallulah Bankhead, American actress and bonne vivante

Keep a diary and one day it'll keep you.

> Mae West, American actress

I never travel without my diary. One should always have something sensational to read in the train.

> Oscar Wilde, *The Importance of Being Earnest* (1895)

See also #AUTOBIOGRAPHY, #BIOGRAPHY

#DICKENS, CHARLES
1812–70, English writer and social critic

He describes London like a special correspondent for posterity.

> Walter Bagehot, *National Review*, 1858

We were put to Dickens as children but it never quite took off. That unremitting humanity soon had me cheesed off.

    Alan Bennett, *The Old Country* (1978)

About a year ago, from idle curiosity, I picked up *The Old Curiosity Shop*, and of all the rotten vulgar un-literary writing...! Worse than George Eliot's. If a novelist can't write where is the beggar.

    Arnold Bennett, English author and journalist

Not much of Dickens will live, because it has so little correspondence to life ... If his novels are read at all in the future, people will wonder what we saw in them, save some possible element of fun meaningless to them.

    George Meredith, English novelist and poet

He has never played any significant part in any movement more significant than that of a fly on a wheel.

    Saturday Review

Of Dickens's style, it is impossible to speak in praise. It is jerky, ungrammatical and created by himself in defiance of rules.

    Anthony Trollope, English novelist

I have no sense of humor. In illustration of this fact I will say this – by way of confession – that if there is a humorous passage in the *Pickwick Papers*, I have never been able to find it.

    Mark Twain, American author and humorist

One must have a heart of stone to read the death of Little Nell without laughing.

Oscar Wilde, Irish writer, essayist and playwright

#DICTIONARIES

See #REFERENCE

E

#E-BOOKS

See #KINDLE, THE

#ENGLISH LANGUAGE, THE

Is there a word in the English language which contains
all the vowels?
    Unquestionably.
    Anon.

A spelling reformer indicted
For fudge was before the court cicted.
The judge said: 'Enough–
His candle we'll snough,
And his sepulcher shall not be whicted.
    Anon., cited in A. Bierce, *The Devil's Dictionary*
    (1911)

Stylists used to revere 'pure' English but in reality
English is about as pure as a factory effluent and has

displayed its mongrel toughness over the centuries by cannibalising a picturesque array of foreign tongues from Greek to Polynesian.

John Carey, *Sunday Times*, 1985

The most dreaded words in the English language are: 'Some assembly required.'

Bill Cosby, American comedian

Trevor realized that the odd thing about English is that no matter how much you screw sequences word up up, you understood, still, like Yoda, will be. Other languages don't work that way. French? *Dieu!* Misplace a single *le* or *la* and an idea vaporizes into a sonic puff. English is flexible: you can jam it into a Cuisinart for an hour, remove it, and meaning will still emerge.

Douglas Coupland, *Generation A* (2009)

The English language is a work in progress. Have fun with it.

Jonathan Culver, American writer

Even if you do learn to speak correct English, whom are you going to speak it to?

Clarence Darrow, American lawyer

When the American people get through with the English language, it will look as if it had been run over by a musical comedy.

Finley Peter Dunne, *Mr Dooley at his Best* (1938)

People who start a sentence with personally (and they're always women) ought to be thrown to the lions. It's a repulsive habit.
  Georgette Heyer, *Death in the Stocks* (1935)

The English language was carefully, carefully cobbled together by three blind dudes and a German dictionary.
  Dave Kellett, American writer and cartoonist

(In England) a fishmonger is a man who mongs fish; the ironmonger and the warmonger do the same with iron and war. They just mong them.
  George Mikes, *How to be an Alien* (1946)

English doesn't borrow from other languages. English follows other languages down dark alleys, knocks them over and goes through their pockets for loose grammar.
  James Nicoll, Canadian author of the epigram 'The Purity of the English Language' (1990)

If I've told you once, I've told you a thousand times, resist hyperbole.
  William Safire, American author and presidential speechwriter

Never use a long word when a diminutive one will do.
  William Safire

The worst words in the English language are, 'We have to talk.'

Either that or, 'Whose bra is this?'

Jerry Seinfeld, American comedian

The English have no respect for their language, and will not teach their children to speak it.

George Bernard Shaw, preface to *Pygmalion* (1912)

No modern literary work of any worth has been produced in the English language by an English writer – except, of course, Bradshaw.

Oscar Wilde, Irish writer, essayist and playwright, on the legendary railway guide

See also #GRAMMAR, #WORDS

#EPIGRAMS

Epigram and truth are rarely commensurate. Truth has to be somewhat chiselled, as it were, before it will fit into an epigram.

Joseph Farrell, *Lectures of a Certain Professor* (1877)

An epigram is only a wisecrack that's played Carnegie Hall.

Oscar Levant, American composer, author and actor

See also #QUOTATIONS

#EPITAPHS

When I am dead, I hope it may be said,
'His sins were scarlet, but his books were read.'
  Hilaire Belloc, 'On His Books' (1923)

ERNIE: What would you like them to put on your tombstone?
ERIC: Something short and simple.
ERNIE: What?
ERIC: 'Back in Five Minutes.'
  Cited in E. Braben, *The Best of Morecambe and Wise* (1974)

I Would Rather Be Living in Philadelphia
  W. C. Fields, suggested epitaph for himself, *Vanity Fair*, 1925

Over my dead body!
  George F. Kaufman, suggested epitaph for himself, *Vanity Fair*, 1925

Excuse My Dust
  Dorothy Parker, suggested epitaph for herself, *Vanity Fair*, 1925

See also #LAST WORDS, #OBITUARIES

F

#FAILURE

There is much to be said for failure. It is more interesting than success.
 Max Beerbohm, *Mainly on the Air* (1946)

Writers are always envious, mean minded, filled with rage and envy at others' good fortune. There is nothing like the failure of a close friend to cheer us up.
 Peter Carey, Australian novelist, 2002

That poor man. He's completely unspoiled by failure.
 Noël Coward, English playwright and entertainer, of
 a fellow playwright

I had a boyfriend who told me I'd never succeed, never be nominated for a Grammy, never have a hit song, and that he hoped I'd fail. I said to him, 'Someday, when we're not together, you won't be able to order a cup of coffee at the fucking deli without hearing or seeing me.'
 Lady Gaga, American pop singer

There is the greatest practical benefit in making a few failures early in life.
    T. H. Huxley, 'On Medical Education' (1870)

Failure has gone to his head.
    Wilson Mizner, American playwright and raconteur,
    of a still-buoyant bankrupt

If I were not a gloriously successful person, in England they would have dismissed me as an Irishman and in America as a Socialist.
    George Bernard Shaw, Irish playwright

It is not enough to succeed. Others must fail.
    Gore Vidal, American critic and commentator

See also #SUCCESS

#FAME

A celebrity is someone who works all his life to become known, then wears dark glasses to avoid being recognised.
    Fred Allen, American comedian

Fame is when you're known by people you don't know.
    Anon.

The first test of fame is to have a crazy person imagine he is you.
Anon.

When you're the toast of the town, everyone wants to butter you up.
Anon.

Darling, I have enemies I've never met. That's fame!
Tallulah Bankhead, American actress and bonne vivante

He is remembered chiefly as the man about whom all is forgotten.
Nicolas Bentley, English author and illustrator

Glory is fleeting, but obscurity is forever.
Napoleon Bonaparte, French military and political leader

In the march up to the heights of fame there comes a spot close to the summit in which a man reads nothing but detective stories.
Heywood Broun, American wit

Happy is the man who hath never known what it is to taste of fame – to have it is a purgatory, to want it is a Hell.
Edward Bulwer-Lytton, English poet, playwright and politician

Fame is being asked to sign your autograph on the back of a cigarette packet.

    Billy Connolly, Scottish comedian

My reputation is terrible, which comforts me a lot.

    Noël Coward, English playwright and entertainer

He's very, very well known. I'd say he's world-famous in Melbourne.

    Dame Edna Everage (Barry Humphries), *Russell Harty Plus*, London Weekend Television, 1973

The nice thing about being a celebrity is that when you bore people, they think it's their fault.

    Henry Kissinger, American diplomat

The best fame is a writer's fame; it's enough to get you a table at a good restaurant, but not enough that you get interrupted when you eat.

    Fran Lebowitz, American author and commentator, 1993

One of the drawbacks of fame is that one can never escape from it.

    Nellie Melba, Australian operatic soprano

First you're an unknown, then you write one book and you move up to obscurity.

    Martin Myers, author and wit

The distance from obscurity to fame is much longer than from fame to obscurity.

    It's a short walk from the hallelujah to the hoot.

    Vladimir Nabokov, Russian novelist

I was the toast of two continents: Greenland and Australia.

    Dorothy Parker, American wit

We can't all be heroes. Someone has to sit on the kerb and clap as they go by.

    Will Rogers, American humorist

There are pluses and minuses to fame. The plus is that I am known by everybody. The minus is that I am known by everybody.

    Jerry Springer, American television talk show host

For me I never cared for fame
Solvency was my only aim.

    J. C. Squire, English poet and editor, 1932

Even for learned men, love of fame is the last thing to be given up.

    Tacitus, Roman senator and historian

I always wanted to be somebody, but now I realize I should have been more specific.

    Lily Tomlin, American actress, comedian and writer

The only man who wasn't spoiled by being lionised was Daniel.

    Herbert Beerbohm Tree, English actor and theatre manager

What a heavy burden is a name that has become too famous.

    Voltaire, French writer, historian and philosopher

Fools admire everything in a respected author.

    Voltaire, *Candide* (1759)

In the future, everyone will be famous for fifteen minutes.

    Andy Warhol, American pop artist, 1960s

There is only one thing in the world worse than being talked about and that is not being talked about.

    Oscar Wilde, Irish writer, essayist and playwright

See also #SUCCESS

#FICTION

The difference between reality and fiction is that fiction has to make sense.

    Tom Clancy, American novelist

Good fiction is made of what is real, and reality is difficult to come by.
Ralph Ellison, American novelist

Serious modern fiction has only one subject: the difficulty of writing serious modern fiction.
John Fowles, *Mantissa* (1982)

As a rule reading fiction is as hard to me as trying to hit a target by hurling feathers at it. I need *resistance* to celebrate!
William James, American philosopher

Fiction is a lie, and good fiction is the truth inside the lie.
Stephen King, American novelist

Truth may be stranger than fiction. But fiction is truer.
Frederic Raphael, English novelist

Fiction writing is great. You can make up almost anything.
Ivana Trump, socialite and 'novelist'

Truth is stranger than fiction, but it is because Fiction is obliged to stick to possibilities. Truth isn't.
Mark Twain, *Following the Equator* (1897)

Fiction reveals truths that reality obscures.
Jessamyn West, American novelist

The good ended happily, and the bad unhappily. That is what fiction means.

    Oscar Wilde, Irish writer, essayist and playwright

See also #BESTSELLERS, #PROSE, #WRITERS

#FILM

See #HOLLYWOOD

G

#GRAMMAR

Paragraphing is one of the lower forms of cunning, like a way with women.
  Anon.

Bugger the adjectives. It's the nouns and verbs that people want.
  Anon.

This is the type of arrant pedantry up with which I will not put.
  Anon., *Strand Magazine*; often erroneously attributed to Sir Winston Churchill

Ending a sentence with a preposition is something up with which I will not put.
  Sir Winston Churchill, British Prime Minister 1940–45, 1951–5 (attrib.)

A synonym is a word you use when you can't spell the word you first thought of.
  Burt Bacharach, American songwriter

The personal pronoun in English has three cases, the dominative, the objectionable and the oppressive.
  Ambrose Bierce, American author and critic

... when I split an infinitive, God damn it, I split it so it will stay split.
  Raymond Chandler, American novelist and screen-
  writer, letter, 1947

It never ceases to amaze me how prosaic, pedestrian, unimaginative people can persistently pontificate about classical grammatical structure as though it's fucking rocket science. These must be the same people who hate Picasso, because he couldn't keep the paint inside the lines and the colors never matched the numbers.
  Abbe Diaz, American socialite

I don't split 'em. When I go to work on an infinitive, I break it up in little pieces.
  Jimmy Durante, American comedian and singer

Correct English is the slang of prigs who write history and essays.
  George Eliot, *Middlemarch* (1874)

The adjective is the banana peel of the parts of speech.
  Clifton Fadiman, *Reader's Digest*, 1956

Women are the simple, and poets the superior, artisans of language ... the intervention of grammarians is almost always bad.

Rémy de Gourmont, French poet, novelist and critic

I adore adverbs; they are the only qualifications I really much respect.

Henry James, American novelist

What really alarms me about President Bush's 'War on Terrorism' is the grammar. How do you wage war on an abstract noun? How is 'Terrorism' going to surrender? It's well known, in philological circles, that it's very hard for abstract nouns to surrender.

Terry Jones, Welsh actor and wit

The greater part of the world's troubles are due to questions of grammar.

Michel de Montaigne, French Renaissance writer, *The Complete Essays*

The past is always tense, the future perfect.

Zadie Smith, English novelist

Word has somehow got around that the split infinitive is always wrong. That is a piece with the outworn notion that it is always wrong to strike a lady.

James Thurber, American comic writer

Ignorant people think it is the noise which fighting cats make that is so aggravating, but it ain't so; it is the sickening grammar that they use.
   Mark Twain, American author and humorist

'Which is him?' The grammar was faulty, maybe, but we could not know, then, that it would go in a book someday.
   Mark Twain, *Roughing It* (1872)

As to the Adjective, when in doubt, strike it out.
   Mark Twain, *Pudd'nhead Wilson* (1894)

Damn the subjunctive. It brings all our writers to shame.
   Mark Twain, *Notebook* (1935), ed. by Albert Bigelow
   Paine

Why is the alphabet in that order? Is it because of the song?
   Steven Wright, American comedian

See also #LANGUAGE

#GREAT WRITERS

George Bernard Shaw's handwriting was exquisite – like a fly which had been trained at the Russian ballet.
   James Agate, English diarist and critic

Children swarmed to him like settlers. He became a land.
  W. H. Auden, Anglo-American poet, on English poet
  and artist Edward Lear, 1939

A man who has not read Homer is like a man who has
not seen the ocean. There is a great object of which he
has no idea.
  Walter Bagehot, English journalist and essayist

Thackeray is like the edited and illustrated edition of
a great dinner.
  Walter Bagehot, *The Spectator*, 1862

Agatha Christie has given more pleasure in bed than
any other woman.
  Nancy Banks-Smith, English journalist and critic

Chesterton had a body like a slag heap but a mind like
the dawn sky. He saw the world new, as if he'd just
landed from another planet.
  John Carey, English critic, on G. K. Chesterton,
  English author, *Sunday Times*, 1978

Betjeman's cachet is by now that of a cherished public
monument. It would be only mildly surprising to hear
that he had been acquired by the National Trust.
  John Carey, on John Betjeman, English poet, 1983

He is both glum and funny, a mixture the English always find endearing.

John Carey, on Alan Bennett, English diarist and playwright, 1994

He wrote like God. He could put words together with such certainty that they seem to have been graven on tablets of stone from the beginning of time.

John Carey, on W. B. Yeats, Irish poet and literary figure, 2000

Whatever Wells writes is not only alive, but kicking.

Henry James, American novelist, on H. G. Wells, English novelist, historian and commentator, 1936

He was dull in a new way that made people think him great.

Samuel Johnson, English poet, biographer and lexicographer, on English poet Thomas Gray, 1775

On the day that God made Carl Sandburg, he didn't do anything else that day but feel good.

Edward Steichen, photographer and painter, on the American editor and poet.

I can never remember if Moby Dick is the man or the whale.

James Thurber, American comic writer

He is a most remarkable man – and I am the other one. Between us we cover all knowledge; he knows all that can be known and I know the rest.

Mark Twain, American author and humorist, on English writer and poet Rudyard Kipling, 1924

See also #WRITERS ON WRITERS

H

#HEMINGWAY, ERNEST
1899–1961, American author and journalist

He has never been known to use a word that might send a man to a dictionary.
William Faulkner, American novelist

… always willing to lend a helping hand to the one above him.
F. Scott Fitzgerald, American novelist

A man must be a very great genius to make up for being such a loathsome human being.
Martha Gellhorn, American journalist and travel writer

He's got hold of the red meat of the English language and turned it into hamburgers.
Richard Gordon, English novelist and screenwriter

What was special about Ernest Hemingway was his insistence that all his wives should learn to shoot straight.
  Mary Hemingway, journalist and fourth wife of
  Ernest Hemingway

As to Hemingway, I read him for the first time in the early '40s, something about bells, balls and bulls, and loathed it.
  Vladimir Nabokov, Russian novelist

What other culture could have produced someone like Hemingway and *not* seen the joke?
  Gore Vidal, American critic and commentator

Take Hemingway. People always think that the reason he's easy to read is that he is concise. He isn't. I hate conciseness – it's too difficult. The reason Hemingway is easy to read is that he repeats himself all the time, using 'and' for padding.
  Tom Wolfe, American novelist and commentator

#HISTORY

Historian: A broad-gauge gossip.
  Ambrose Bierce, *The Devil's Dictionary* (1911)

History: An account mostly false, of events mostly unimportant, which are brought about by rulers mostly knaves, and soldiers mostly fools.
  Ambrose Bierce, *The Devil's Dictionary* (1911)

History is the version of past events that people have decided to agree upon.
  Napoleon Bonaparte, French military and political leader

History will be kind to me for I intend to write it.
  Sir Winston Churchill, British Prime Minister 1940–45, 1951–5

History is more or less bunk. It's tradition. We don't want tradition. We want to live in the present and the only history that is worth a tinker's damn is the history we made today.
  Henry Ford, American car maker, in an interview, 1916

It takes a great deal of history to produce a little literature.
  Henry James, *Nathaniel Hawthorne* (1896)

Perhaps nobody has changed the course of history as much as the historians.
  Franklin P. Jones, American journalist and humorist

A historian is often only a journalist facing backwards.
  Karl Kraus, Austrian writer and aphorist

Historian: an unsuccessful novelist.
  H. L. Mencken, American humorist

History is a pack of lies about events that never happened told by people who weren't there.
George Santayana, Spanish-born philosopher, author and poet

For four-fifths of our history, our planet was populated by pond scum.
J. W. Schopf, American scientist

History knows that it can wait for more evidence and review its older verdicts; it offers an endless series of courts of appeal, and is ever ready to reopen closed cases.
William Stubbs, English historian and Bishop of Oxford

History is the propaganda of the victors.
Ernst Toller, German playwright

It might be a good idea if the various countries of the world would occasionally swap history books, just to see what other people are doing with the same set of facts.
Bill Vaughn, American columnist and author

#HOLLYWOOD

You can take all the sincerity in Hollywood, place it in the navel of a fruit fly and still have room enough for three caraway seeds and a producer's heart.
Fred Allen, American comedian

An associate producer is the only guy in Hollywood who will associate with a producer.
    Fred Allen

Hollywood is not only dog eat dog; it's dog doesn't return other dog's phonecalls.
    Woody Allen, American film-maker and actor

The thing about Hollywood is, you have to be grateful to be working with thieves and liars. Because the alternative is idiots.
    David Ambrose, English writer

In Hollywood, if you don't have a psychiatrist, people think you're crazy.
    Anon.

They had a quiet Hollywood wedding. Only the press agents of the immediate family were present.
    Anon.

You're no one in Hollywood unless somebody wants you dead.
    Bernie Brillstein, American producer

Giving your book to Hollywood is like pimping your daughter.
    Tom Clancy, American novelist

In Hollywood they only know one word of more than one syllable. And that's 'fillum'.
    Jerry Dennis, English comedian

I read part of it all the way through.
    Samuel Goldwyn, American film mogul

In two words: im possible.
    Samuel Goldwyn

Having your book turned into a movie is like seeing your oxen turned into bouillon cubes.
    John le Carré, English author

Seeing your book turned into a movie is like watching your children get raped by Cossacks.
    Kathy Lette, Australian novelist

It's an opportunity to fly first class, be treated like a celebrity, sit around the pool and be betrayed.
    Ian McEwan, English novelist, on working in
    Hollywood

Hollywood ... a delightful trip through a sewer in a glass-bottomed boat.
    Wilson Mizner, American playwright and raconteur

Working for Warner Brothers is like fucking a porcupine; it's 100 pricks against one.
    Wilson Mizner

The only 'ism' Hollywood believes in is plagiarism.
   Dorothy Parker, American wit

In Hollywood it's not how you play the game; it's how you place the blame.
   Don Simpson, American producer

I'm A Writer But Then Nobody's Perfect
   Billy Wilder, American film writer, epitaph

#HUMOUR

Caustic: adjective applied to the wit of magistrates and judges, as in the sentence, 'The judge then asked who was this gentleman, Mussolini, who appeared to be an Italian?'
   J. B. Morton (Beachcomber), *Beachcomber: The Works of J. B. Morton*, (1974) ed. by R. Ingrams

Defining and analyzing humor is a pastime of humorless people.
   Robert Benchley, American humorist

Mark my words, when a society has to resort to the lavatory for its humour, the writing is on the wall.
   Alan Bennett, *Forty Years On* (1968)

There is a thin line that separates laughter and pain, comedy and tragedy, humor and hurt.
   Erma Bombeck, American humorist

There's no possibility of being witty without a little ill-nature.
     Richard Brinsley Sheridan, Irish playwright and poet

A rich man's joke is always funny.
     Heywood Broun, American writer

Wit ought to be a glorious treat, like caviar; never spread it around like marmalade.
     Noël Coward, English playwright and entertainer

The satirist shoots to kill while the humorist brings his prey back alive and eventually releases him again for another chance.
     Peter De Vries, American novelist

There is nothing in the world so irresistibly contagious as laughter and good humour.
     Charles Dickens, *A Christmas Carol* (1843)

A difference of taste in jokes is a great strain on the affections.
     George Eliot, English novelist

Forgive, O Lord, my little jokes on Thee
And I'll forgive Thy great big one on me.
     Robert Frost, American poet

There is no reason why a joke should not be appreciated more than once. Imagine how little good music there would be if, for example, a conductor refused to play Beethoven's Fifth Symphony on the ground that his audience might have heard it before.

A. P. Herbert, English wit

Life doesn't make any sense, and we all pretend it does. Comedy's job is to point out that it doesn't make sense, and that it doesn't make much difference anyway.

Eric Idle, English writer and comedian

Laughter gives us distance. It allows us to step back from an event, deal with it and then move on.

Bob Newhart, American comedian

A joke was not a single-use item but something you brought out again and again until it fell apart in your hand like a cheap umbrella.

David Nicholls, English novelist and screenwriter

Humour is the shock absorber of life; it helps us take the blows.

Peggy Noonan, American presidential speechwriter

Practically anything you say will seem amusing if you say it on all fours.

P. J. O'Rourke, American satirist

Wits have one thing in common with bores: they recognise at sight and avoid one another, fearing competition.

Hesketh Pearson, *Lives of the Wits* (1962)

Everything is funny as long as it is happening to somebody else.

Will Rogers, American humorist

There's no trick to being a humorist when you have the whole government working for you.

Will Rogers

Humour is, I think, the subtlest and chanciest of literary forms. It is surely not accidental that there are a thousand novelists, essayists, poets or journalists for each humorist. It is a long, long time between James Thurbers.

Leo Rosten, American humorist

Nothing is more curious than the almost savage hostility that humour excites in those who lack it.

George Saintsbury, English writer, scholar and critic

Non-participation on the part of the recipient of the pastry is the chief ingredient of the recipe for successful custard-pie throwing.

Mack Sennett, American film director

When a thing is funny, search it for a hidden truth.

George Bernard Shaw, Irish playwright

My way of joking is to tell the truth. It's the funniest joke in the world.
> George Bernard Shaw, *John Bull's Other Island* (1904)

Humor is emotional chaos remembered in tranquility.
> James Thurber, American comic writer

The wit makes fun of other persons; the satirist makes fun of the world; the humorist makes fun of himself.
> James Thurber, in a TV interview

Wit is the sudden marriage of ideas which, before their union, were not perceived to have any relation.
> Mark Twain, *Notebook* (1935), ed. by Albert Bigelow Paine

Humor keeps us alive. Humor and food. Don't forget food. You can go a week without laughing.
> Joss Whedon, American screenwriter, producer and comic book author

Humor can be dissected, as a frog can, but the thing dies in the process and the innards are discouraging to any but the pure scientific mind.
> E. B. White, introduction to *A Subtreasury of American Humor* (1941)

Nothing spoils a romance so much as a sense of humour in the woman – or the want of it in a man.
> Oscar Wilde, *A Woman of No Importance* (1893)

See also #SATIRE

I

#ILLITERACY

Do you ever wonder if illiterate people get the full effect of alphabet soup?
  John Mendoza, American comedian

#INSPIRATION

Inspiration is for amateurs, I just get to work.
  Chuck Close, American painter and photographer

J

#JAMES, HENRY
1843–1916, American writer

It took me years to ascertain that Henry James's work was giving me little pleasure ... In each case I asked myself: 'What the dickens is this novel about, and where does it think it's going to?' Question unanswerable! I gave up. Today I have no recollection whatever of any characters or any events in either novel.
  Arnold Bennett, English author and journalist

... had a mind so fine that no idea could violate it.
  T. S. Eliot, American poet and critic

... one of the nicest old ladies I ever met.
  William Faulkner, American novelist

Henry James had turned his back on one of the great events in the world's history, the rise of the United States, in order to report tittle-tattle at tea parties in English country houses.
  W. Somerset Maugham, English playwright, novelist and short story writer, on American novelist Henry James

The death of a member of the lower classes could be trusted to give him a good chuckle.
W. Somerset Maugham, on American novelist
Henry James

... a little, emasculated mass of inanity.
Theodore Roosevelt, US President 1901–09

Once you've put one of his books down, you simply can't pick it up again.
Mark Twain, American author and humorist

Bare verbs he rarely tolerates. He splits infinitives and fills them up with adverbial stuffing. He presses the passing colloquialism into his service. His vast paragraphs sweat and struggle.
H. G. Wells, English novelist, historian and
commentator

Mr Henry James writes fiction as if it were a painful duty.
Oscar Wilde, 'The Decay of Lying' (1891)

#JEALOUSY

The dullard's envy of brilliant men is always assuaged by the suspicion that they will come to a bad end.
Max Beerbohm, *Zuleika Dobson* (1911)

Calamities are of two kinds: misfortune to ourselves, and good fortune to others.

Ambrose Bierce, American author and critic

Our envy always lasts longer than the happiness of those we envy.

François de La Rochefoucauld, French author and memoirist

Anybody can sympathise with the sufferings of a friend, but it requires a very fine nature to sympathise with a friend's success.

Oscar Wilde, 'The Soul of Man under Socialism' (1891)

He was a man of strong passions, and the green-eyed monster ran up his leg and bit him to the bone.

P. G. Wodehouse, *Full Moon* (1947)

#JOURNALISM

Sex Change Archbishop in Mercy Palace Dash

Anon. (the perfect tabloid headline)

Trying to be a first-rate reporter on the average American newspaper is like trying to play Bach's 'St Matthew's Passion' on a ukulele.

Ben Bagdikian, American author and journalist

Anyone Here Been Raped and Speaks English?
  Edward Behr, British foreign correspondent and war
  journalist, proposing a book title, 1978. Inspired by
  an incident at an airport in the Congo, when a British
  TV reporter allegedly approached groups of Belgian
  refugees fleeing from rebel troops with this question

No news is good news; no journalists is even better.
  Nicolas Bentley, English author and illustrator

The newspapers! Sir, they are the most villainous –
licentious – abominable – infernal – not that I ever
read them – No – I make it a rule never to look into a
newspaper.
  Richard Brinsley Sheridan, *The Critic*, 1779

It was long ago in my life as a simple reporter that I
decided that facts must never get in the way of truth.
  James Cameron, English journalist

Journalism largely consists in saying 'Lord Jones Dead'
to people who never knew Lord Jones was alive.
  G. K. Chesterton, *The Wisdom of Father Brown* (1914)

Literature is the art of writing something that will be
read twice; journalism what will be read once.
  Cyril Connolly, *Enemies of Promise* (1938)

The man who reads nothing at all is better educated
than the man who reads nothing but newspapers.
  Thomas Jefferson, US President 1801–9

The secret of successful journalism is to make your readers so angry they will write half your paper for you.
    C. E. M. Joad, English philosopher and broadcaster

Cronyism is the curse of journalism. After many years I have reached the firm conclusion that it is impossible for any objective newspaperman to be a friend of a President.
    Walter Lippmann, American writer

If a person is not talented enough to be a novelist, not smart enough to be a lawyer, and his hands are too shaky to perform operations, he becomes a journalist.
    Norman Mailer, American writer and film-maker

The art of newspaper paragraphing is to stroke a platitude until it purrs like an epigram.
    Don Marquis, American humorist

A foreign correspondent is someone who lives in foreign parts and corresponds, usually in the form of essays containing no new facts. Otherwise he's someone who flies around from hotel to hotel and thinks that the most interesting thing about any story is the fact that he has arrived to cover it.
    Tom Stoppard, *Night and Day* (1978)

RUTH: Perhaps I'll get him a reporter doll for Christmas. Wind it up and it gets it wrong. What does it say when you press its stomach? Come on, Dick!
DICK: I name the guilty man.
    Tom Stoppard, *Night and Day* (1978)

The only qualities essential for real success in journalism are ratlike cunning, a plausible manner and a little literary ability ... the capacity to steal other people's ideas and phrases ... is also invaluable.

Nicholas Tomalin, English journalist

There are only two forces that can carry light to all corners of the globe – the sun in the heavens and the Associated Press.

Mark Twain, speech to the Annual Dinner of the
Associated Press, New York, 1906

A journalist is somebody who possesses himself of a fantasy and lures the truth towards it.

Arnold Wesker, *Journey into Journalism* (1977)

There is much to be said in favour of modern journalism. By giving us the opinions of the uneducated, it keeps us in touch with the ignorance of the community.

Oscar Wilde, 'The Critic as Artist' (1890)

The public have an insatiable curiosity to know everything. Except what is worth knowing. Journalism, conscious of this, and having tradesman-like habits, supplies their demands.

Oscar Wilde, 'The Soul of Man under Socialism' (1891)

With regard to modern journalists, they always apologise to one in private for what they have written against one in public.

Oscar Wilde, 'The Soul of Man under Socialism' (1891)

You cannot hope to bribe or twist,
thank God! the
British journalist.
But, seeing what
the man will do
unbribed, there's
no occasion to.

Humbert Wolfe, 'Over the Fire', *The Uncelestial City*
(1930)

K

#KINDLE, THE

Until recently, I was an ebook sceptic, see; one of those people who harrumphs about the 'physical pleasure of turning actual pages' and how ebooks will 'never replace the real thing'. Then I was given a Kindle as a present. That shut me up. Stock complaints about the inherent pleasure of ye olde format are bandied about whenever some new upstart invention comes along. Each moan is nothing more than a little foetus of nostalgia jerking in your gut. First they said CDs were no match for vinyl. Then they said MP3s were no match for CDs. Now they say streaming music services are no match for MP3s. They're only happy looking in the rear-view mirror.

Charlie Brooker, English columnist, *The Guardian*

My Kindle reads to me *50 Shades of Grey*. It's like having an obscene phone call from Professor Stephen Hawking.

Jerry Dennis, English comedian

Books are no more threatened by Kindle than stairs by elevators.

  Stephen Fry, English actor, writer and presenter

A crazy certainty had arisen in his mind: a hand – or perhaps a claw – was going to swim up from the grayness of the Kindle's screen, grab him by the throat, and yank him in.

  Stephen King, American novelist

It seems to me that anyone whose library consists of a Kindle lying on a table is some sort of bloodless nerd.

  Penelope Lively, English novelist

The big advantage of a book is it's very easy to rewind. Close it and you're right back at the beginning.

  Jerry Seinfeld, American comedian

L

#LANGUAGE

Remember, double negatives are a complete no-no.
  Anon.

TEACHER: Although a double negative is taken to mean an affirmative, a double affirmative is never taken to mean a negative.
STUDENT: Yeah, right!
  Anon.

Why is 'abbreviation' such a long word?
  Anon.

Apart from a few odd words in Hebrew, I take it completely for granted that God has never spoken anything but the most dignified English.
  Clarence Day, American author

Correct English is the slang of prigs who write history and essays. And the strongest slang of all is the slang of poets.

George Eliot, *Middlemarch* (1874)

I speak Esperanto like a native.

Spike Milligan, English writer and comedian

Listen, someone's screaming in agony – fortunately I speak it fluently.

Spike Milligan, *The Goon Show*, BBC Radio, 1959

Slang is language that rolls up its sleeves, spits on its hands and goes to work.

Carl Sandburg, American writer and editor, *New York Times*, 1959

Man invented language to satisfy his deep need to complain.

Lily Tomlin, American actress, comedian and writer

In addition to these large rules, there are some little ones. These require that the author shall:

Say what he is proposing to say, not merely come near it.

Use the right word, not its second cousin.

Mark Twain, detailing eighteen rules of fiction, reviewing *The Deerslayer* by James Fenimore Cooper

We have really everything in common with America nowadays, except, of course, language.
  Oscar Wilde, 'The Canterville Ghost' (1887)

A simile committing suicide is always a depressing spectacle.
  Oscar Wilde, *Pall Mall Gazette*, 1887

See also #GRAMMAR

#LAST WORDS

Die, my dear doctor? That's the last thing I shall do.
  Lord Palmerston, English politician, 1865

If this is dying, I don't think much of it.
  Lytton Strachey, English writer and critic, 1932

Either they go, or I do.
  Oscar Wilde, Irish writer, essayist and playwright, of his new bedroom curtains, 1900

TEN FAMOUS LAST WORDS:

1. Pull the pin and count to what?
2. Nice doggie!
3. These are the good kind of mushrooms.
4. Which wire was I supposed to cut?
5. I wonder where the mother bear is.

6.   I'll hold it and you light the fuse.
7.   Hey, that's not a violin!
8.   Well, we've made it this far.
9.   *I'll* get your toast out.
10. Give me liberty or give me death.
      Anon.

See also #EPITAPHS, #OBITUARIES

#LETTERS

The great secret in life ... not to open your letters for a fortnight. At the expiration of that period you will find that nearly all of them have answered themselves.
    Arthur Binstead, *Pitcher's Proverbs* (1900)

He's a distinguished man of letters. He works for the Post Office.
    Max Kauffman, comedian

To the Editor of *The Times*
Sir,
I have just written you a long letter.
    On reading it over, I have thrown it into the waste-paper basket.
    Hoping this will meet with your approval. I am Sir
    Your obedient servant
    Lt Col. A. D. Wintle, unpublished letter to *The Times*, 1946

What a girl! He had never in his life before met a woman who could write a letter without a postscript, and this was but the smallest of her unusual gifts.

P. G. Wodehouse, *A Damsel in Distress* (1919)

#LIBRARIES

My sister is a librarian. She carries a card that reads: IN CASE OF EMERGENCY, SSHHHH!

Anon.

I'm fanatically tidy. I may only have one book in my library but at least it's in alphabetical order!

Anon.

Being a librarian doesn't help. I've always found them close relatives of the living dead.

Alan Bennett, 'Instead of a Present', *Larkin at Sixty* (1982)

I have always imagined that Paradise will be a kind of library.

Jorge Luis Borges, Argentinian essayist and poet

'Children, don't speak so coarsely,' said Mr Webster, who had a vague notion that some supervision should be exercised over his daughters' speech, and that a line should be drawn, but never knew quite when to draw it. He had allowed his daughters to use his library without restraint, and nothing is more fatal

to maidenly delicacy of speech than the run of a good library.
    Robertson Davies, *Tempest-Tost* (1951)

No place affords a more striking conviction of the vanity of human hopes, than a public library.
    Samuel Johnson, English poet, biographer and
    lexicographer

There are 70 million books in American libraries, but the one you want is always out.
    Tom Masson, American editor and author

The library is the room in a country house where the murder takes place.
    J. B. Morton, English columnist

The local library was moving to the other side of town. To save costs, residents were asked to help out by borrowing ten books each and returning them three weeks later.
    Sally Poplin, English writer

The Librarian was, of course, very much in favour of reading in general, but readers in particular ... He liked people who loved and respected books, and the best way to do that, in the Librarian's opinion, was to leave them on the shelves where nature intended them to be.
    Terry Pratchett, *Men at Arms* (1993)

See also #BOOKS

#LIMERICKS

The limerick packs laughs anatomical
Into space that is quite economical.
But the good ones I've seen
So seldom are clean
And the clean ones so seldom are comical.
　　Anon.

There was a young man from Peru
Whose limericks stopped at line two.
　　Anon.

The limerick's an art-form complex
Whose contents run chiefly to sex.
It's famous for virgins
And masculine urgin's
And vulgar erotic effects.
　　Anon., cited in W. S. Baring-Gould, *The Lure of the
　　Limerick* (1967)

Well, it's partly the shape of the thing
That gives the old limerick wing;
These accordian pleats
Full of airy conceits
Take it up like a kite on a string.
　　Anon., cited in W. S. Baring-Gould, *The Lure of the
　　Limerick* (1967)

Most women loathe limericks, for the same reason that calves hate cookbooks.
    Gershon Legman, American critic and folklorist

There are three kinds of limericks: limericks when ladies are present, limericks when ladies are absent but clergymen are present, and limericks.
    Don Marquis, American humorist

The limerick, peculiar to English,
Is a verse form that's hard to extinguish.
Once Congress in session
Decreed its suppression
But people got around it by writing the last line without any rhyme or meter.
    Professor T. J. Spencer (attrib.)

See also #POETS AND POETRY

#LITERARY INSULTS

There is nothing as rare as a Woollcott first edition, except perhaps a Woollcott *second* edition.
    Franklin P. Adams, American journalist, on Alexander
    Woollcott, *New Yorker* critic and commentator

For in point of style, or manner, or whatever, it is diffi-
cult to imagine anything much worse than the prose of
Mr Pound. It is ugliness and awkwardness incarnate.
Did he always write so badly?

Conrad Aiken, American writer, on Ezra Pound,
American poet and critic

Vidal gives the impression of believing that the entire
heterosexual edifice – registry offices, *Romeo and
Juliet,* the disposable diaper – is just a sorry story of
self-hypnosis and mass hysteria: a hoax, a racket, or
sheer propaganda.

Martin Amis, English novelist, on Gore Vidal,
American critic and commentator

Reading *Don Quixote* can be compared to an indefi-
nite visit from your most impossible senior relative,
with all his pranks, dirty habits, unstoppable reminis-
cences, and terrible cronies. When the experience is
over, and the old boy checks out at last (on page 846
– the prose wedged tight, with no breaks for dialogue),
you will shed tears all right; not tears of relief or regret
but tears of pride. You made it, despite all that *Don
Quixote* could do.

Martin Amis, on Miguel Cervantes, Spanish novelist,
poet and playwright

Walt Whitman is as unacquainted with art as a hog
with mathematics.

Anon.

I hate authors. I wouldn't mind them so much if they
didn't write books.

    Elizabeth von Arnim, British novelist

An unmanly sort of man whose love-life seems to have
been largely confined to crying in laps and playing
mouse.

    W. H. Auden, Anglo-American poet, on Edgar Allan
    Poe, American poet, critic and editor

A fat little flabby person with the face of a baker,
the clothes of a cobbler, the size of a barrelmaker, the
manners of a stocking salesman and the dress of an
innkeeper.

    Victor de Baladin, on Honoré de Balzac, French novelist

I grow bored in France – and the main reason is
that everybody here resembles Voltaire ... the king
of nincompoops, the prince of the superficial, the
anti-artist, the spokesman of janitresses, the Father
Gigone of the editors of Siècle.

    Charles Baudelaire, French poet and essayist, on
    Voltaire, French writer, historian and philosopher

Of course we all know that Morris was a wonderful
all-round man but the act of walking round him has
always tired me.

    Max Beerbohm, English writer and critic, on William
    Morris, English writer, artist and libertarian socialist

So boring you fall asleep halfway through her name.
  Alan Bennett, English diarist and playwright, on
  Arianna Huffington, Greek–American writer and
  columnist

I *hated* [*Catcher in the Rye*]. It took me days to go through it, gingerly, a page at a time, and blushing with embarrassment for him every ridiculous sentence of the way. How can they let him do it?
  Elizabeth Bishop, American author, on J. D. Salinger,
  American novelist and short story writer

How to read *Harry Potter and the Sorcerer's Stone*? Why, very quickly, to begin with, and perhaps also to make an end. Why read it? Presumably, if you cannot be persuaded to read anything better, Rowling will have to do.
  Harold Bloom, American literary critic, on J. K.
  Rowling, English novelist

I have been reading a translation of Goethe's 'Wilhelm Meister'. Is it good? To me it seems perhaps the very worst book I ever read. No Englishman could have written such a book. I cannot remember a single good page or idea ... Is it all a practical joke? If it really is Goethe's 'Wilhelm Meister' that I have been reading, I am glad I have never taken the trouble to learn German.
  Samuel Butler, English author and satirist, on the
  German writer and politician

I guess Gore left the country because he felt that he was underappreciated here. I have news for him: people who actually read his books will underappreciate him everywhere.

Truman Capote, American writer and journalist, on
Gore Vidal, American critic and commentator

Poor Shelley always was, and is, a kind of ghastly object, colourless, pallid, tuneless, without health or warmth or vigour.

Thomas Carlyle, Scottish philosopher, essayist
and historian, on Percy Bysshe Shelley, English
Romantic poet

He has said or done nothing worth a serious man taking the trouble of remembering.

Thomas Carlyle, on Percy Bysshe Shelley

Charles Lamb I sincerely believe to be in some considerable degree insane. A more pitiful, rickety, gasping, staggering, stammering tomfool I do not know. He is witty by denying truisms and abjuring good manners. His speech wriggles hither and thither with an incessant painful fluctuation; not an opinion in it or a fact or even a phrase that you can thank him for.

Thomas Carlyle, on the English essayist

… a hoary-headed and toothless baboon.

Thomas Carlyle, on Algernon Swinburne, English
poet, playwright and critic

Everything he touches smells like a billy goat. He is every kind of writer I detest, a faux naïf, a Proust in greasy overalls.

Raymond Chandler, on fellow American detective fiction writer James M. Cain

He uses a lot of big words, and his sentences are from here to the airport.

Carolyn Chute, American novelist and political activist, on William Faulkner, American novelist

His manners are ninety-nine in a hundred singularly repulsive.

Samuel Taylor Coleridge, English poet, critic and philosopher, on William Hazlitt, English essayist

Let us reflect whether there be any living writer whose silence we would consider to be a literary disaster.

Cyril Connolly, English critic and writer

He could not blow his nose without moralising on the state of the handkerchief industry.

Cyril Connolly, on George Orwell, English writer and commentator, 1968

She looked like Lady Chatterley above the waist and the gamekeeper below

Cyril Connolly, on Vita Sackville-West, English author, poet and gardener

I am fairly unrepentant about her poetry. I really think that three-quarters of it is gibberish. However, I must crush down these thoughts, otherwise the dove of peace will shit on me.

> Noël Coward, English playwright and entertainer, on
> Dame Edith Sitwell, English poet and critic

Frankly my dear, I should bury your script in a drawer and put a lily on top.

> Noël Coward, to an aspiring writer

I can't read ten pages of Steinbeck without throwing up. I couldn't read the proletariat crap that came out in the '30s.

> James Gould Cozzens, American writer, on the
> American novelist

Sometimes when reading Goethe I have the paralyzing suspicion that he is trying to be funny.

> Guy Davenport, American writer and illustrator, on
> the German writer and politician

If it were thought that anything I wrote was influenced by Robert Frost, I would take that particular piece of mine, shred it and flush it down the toilet, hoping not to clog the pipes.

> James Dickey, American poet and novelist, on the
> American poet

He never wrote an invitation to dinner without an eye to posterity.
> Benjamin Disraeli, British Prime Minister 1868, 1874–80, on Edward Bulwer-Lytton, English poet, playwright and politician

An animated adenoid.
> Norman Douglas, English novelist, on Ford Madox Ford, English novelist, poet and critic

I wish her characters would talk a little less like the heroes and heroines of police reports.
> George Eliot, on fellow English novelist Charlotte Brontë

… half song thrush, half alligator.
> Ralph Waldo Emerson, American essayist and poet, on Walt Whitman, American writer

Gertrude Stein was a master at making nothing happen very slowly.
> Clifton Fadiman, American author, editor and broadcaster, on the American novelist and poet

A hack writer who would not have been considered fourth rate in Europe, who tricked out a few of the old proven sure fire literary skeletons with sufficient local color to intrigue the superficial and the lazy.
> William Faulkner, American writer, on Mark Twain, American author and humorist

What an old covered wagon she is.
  F. Scott Fitzgerald, American novelist, on Gertrude
  Stein, American novelist and poet

A great cow full of ink.
  Gustave Flaubert, French novelist, on Georges Sand,
  French novelist and memoirist

What a man Balzac would have been if he had known
how to write.
  Gustave Flaubert, on Honoré de Balzac, French
  novelist

Conrad spent a day finding the *mot juste*, then killed it.
  Ford Madox Ford, English novelist, poet and critic,
  on Polish author Joseph Conrad

She was incredibly ugly, uglier than almost anyone
I had ever met. A thin, withered creature, she sat
hunched in her chair, in her heavy tweed suit and her
thick lisle stockings, impregnable and indifferent. She
had a huge nose, a dark moustache, and her dark-dyed
hair was combed into absurd bangs over her forehead.
  Otto Friedrich, American author and journalist,
  on Alice B. Toklas, American-born member of the
  Parisian avant-garde

There is no arguing with Johnson; for when his pistol misses fire, he knocks you down with the butt-end of it.
> Oliver Goldsmith, Anglo-Irish novelist, poet and playwright, on Samuel Johnson, English poet, biographer and lexicographer

She's genuinely bogus.
> Christopher Hassall, English actor, lyricist and poet, on Dame Edith Sitwell, English poet and critic

Bulwer nauseates me; he is the very pimple of the age's humbug. There is no hope of the public, so long as he retains an admirer, a reader, or a publisher.
> Nathaniel Hawthorne, American novelist and short story writer, on Edward Bulwer-Lytton, English poet, playwright and politician

To me Pound remains the exquisite showman minus the show.
> Ben Hecht, American screenwriter and novelist, on Ezra Pound, American poet and critic

Poor Faulkner. Does he really think big emotions come from big words?
> Ernest Hemingway, on fellow American writer William Faulkner

Have you ever heard of anyone who drank while he worked? You're thinking of Faulkner. He does some-times – and I can tell right in the middle of a page when he's had his first one.
Ernest Hemingway on William Faulkner

He can't write fiction and he can't write non-fiction, so he's invented a bogus category in between.
Ian Hislop, English journalist, broadcaster and sati-rist, on author and former politician Jeffrey Archer's 'novelography'

If you imagine a Scotch commercial traveller in a Scotch commercial hotel leaning on the bar and calling the barmaid Dearie, then you will know the keynote of Burns's verse.
A. E. Housman, English Classical scholar and poet, on Robert Burns, Scottish poet

He saw Jane Austen and Charlotte Brontë as two unpleasant examples of spinsterhood; the one as a prying, sub-acid busybody in everyone else's flirta-tions, the other as a raving, craving maenad seeking self-immolation on the altar of her frustrated passions.
Margaret Irwin, *Bloodstock and Other Stories* (1953)

... a fungus of pendulous shape.
Alice James, American diarist, on George Eliot, English novelist

Barbara Cartland's eyes were two miracles of mascara and looked like two crows that had crashed into a chalk cliff.

>   Clive James, Australian critic, on the English romantic novelist

He was unperfect, unfinished, inartistic; he was worse than provincial – he was parochial.

>   Henry James, American novelist, on Henry David Thoreau, American author and naturalist

An enthusiasm for Poe is the mark of a decidedly primitive stage of reflection.

>   Henry James, on Edgar Allan Poe, American poet, critic and editor

For my part, I can rarely tell whether his characters are making love or playing tennis.

>   Joseph Kraft, syndicated columnist, on William Faulkner, American novelist

Ben Jonson! Not another word about him. It makes my blood boil! I haven't the patience to hear the fellow's name. A pigmy! An upstart! A presumptuous valet who dared to be thought more of than Shakespeare in his day!

>   Walter Savage Landor, English poet and essayist, on Ben Jonson, English playwright, poet and critic

Nobody can be more clownish, more clumsy and sententiously in bad taste, than Herman Melville, even in a great book like *Moby Dick* ... One wearies of the *grand serieux*. There's something false about it. And that's Melville. Oh dear, when the solemn ass brays! brays! brays!

> D. H. Lawrence, English novelist, poet and play-
> wright, on the American writer

My God, what a clumsy olla putrida James Joyce is! Nothing but old fags and cabbage stumps of quotations from the Bible and the rest stewed in the juice of deliberate, journalistic dirty-mindedness.

> D. H. Lawrence, on James Joyce, Irish novelist and poet

The awful Whitman. This post-mortem poet. This poet with the private soul leaking out of him all the time. All his privacy leaking out in a sort of dribble, oozing into the universe.

> D. H. Lawrence, on Walt Whitman, American writer

Spit on her when you see her; she's a liar out and out. As for him, I reserve my language ... vermin, the pair of 'em.

> D. H. Lawrence, on modernist writer Katherine
> Mansfield and English writer J. Middleton Murry

Although Rupert Brooke never succeeded in becoming the first modern poet, he may deserve to be called the first modern undergraduate, a title of comparable significance.
  Michael Levenson, American academic, on the
  English poet

Gertrude Stein's prose-song is a cold black suet-pudding. We can represent it as a cold suet-roll of fabulously reptilian length. Cut it at any point, it is the same thing; the same heavy, sticky, opaque mass all through and all along.
  Wyndham Lewis, English author and painter, on the
  American novelist and poet

A vain, silly, transparent coxcomb without either solid talents or a solid nature.
  J. G. Lockhart, Scottish writer and editor, on Samuel
  Pepys, English diarist

His imagination resembles the wings of an ostrich. It enabled him to run, though not to soar.
  Thomas Babington Macaulay, English historian and
  politician, on John Dryden, English poet, critic and
  playwright

The more I read Socrates, the less I wonder why they poisoned him.
  Thomas Babington Macaulay, on the Greek
  philosopher

I don't like Salinger, not at all. That last thing isn't a novel anyway, whatever it is. I don't like it. Not at all. It suffers from this terrible sort of metropolitan sentimentality and it's so narcissistic. And to me, also, it seemed so false, so calculated. Combining the plain man with an absolutely megalomaniac egotism. I simply can't stand it.

Mary McCarthy, American author, activist and critic, on the American novelist and short story writer

… the white and creamy look of an animated meringue.

Arthur Marshall, English social commentator, on Barbara Cartland, English romantic novelist

Alexander Woollcott looked like something that had gotten loose from the Macy's Thanksgiving Day Parade.

Harpo Marx, actor and comedian, on the *New Yorker* critic and commentator

George Eliot had the heart of Sappho, but the face with the long proboscis, the protruding teeth of the Apocalyptic horse, betrayed animality.

George Meredith, on fellow English novelist

Oscar Wilde's talent seems to me to be essentially rootless, something growing in glass on a little water.

George Moore, Irish poet and novelist, on the Irish writer, essayist and playwright

What is he but the wreck of Stevenson floating about in the slipslop of Henry James?

George Moore, on Polish author Joseph Conrad

... looking himself in his old cloak like a huge umbrella left behind by some picnic party.

George Moore, on W. B. Yeats, Irish poet and
literary figure

Coleridge was a muddle-headed metaphysician who, by some strange streak of fortune, turned out a few real poems amongst the dreary flood of inanity that was his wont. It is these real poems only which must be selected, or we burden the world with another useless book ... There is no difficulty in making the selection – the difference between his poetry and his drivel is so striking.

William Morris, English writer, artist and libertarian
socialist, on Samuel Taylor Coleridge, English poet,
critic and philosopher

Dostoevsky's lack of taste, his monotonous dealings with persons suffering with pre-Freudian complexes, the way he has of wallowing in the tragic misadventures of human dignity – all this is difficult to admire.

Vladimir Nabokov, on fellow Russian novelist
Fyodor Dostoevsky

Actually I loathed the Viennese quack.

Vladimir Nabokov, on Sigmund Freud, Austrian
psychoanalyst

A man who so much resembled a Baked Alaska – sweet, warm and gungy on the outside, hard and cold within.

> Joseph O'Connor, Irish novelist, on C. P. Snow,
> English chemist and novelist

… a sort of gutless Kipling.

> George Orwell, English writer and commentator, on
> W. H. Auden, Anglo-American poet

I invariably miss most of the lines in the last act of an Ibsen play; I always have my fingers in my ears, waiting for the loud report that means that the heroine has just Passed On.

> Dorothy Parker, American wit, on Henrik Ibsen,
> Norwegian poet and playwright

Some of the greatest contributions to English literature have been made by people who have threatened to write a book but have never quite got round to it.

> Sally Poplin, English writer

A great author, notwithstanding his Dictionary is imperfect, his Rambler pompous, his Idler inane, his Lives unjust, his poetry inconsiderable, his learning common, his ideas vulgar, his Irene a child of mediocrity, his genius and wit moderate, his precepts wordly, his politics narrow and his religion bigoted.

> Robert Potter, English critic, on Samuel Johnson,
> English poet, biographer and lexicographer

I believe he creates a milieu in which art is impossible.
Ezra Pound, American poet and critic, on G. K.
Chesterton, English author

... an elderly fallen angel travelling incognito.
Peter Quennell, English writer, on French novelist and
critic André Gide, 1960

To say that Agatha Christie's characters are cardboard
cut-outs is an insult to cardboard cut-outs.
Ruth Rendell, English novelist, on the English
crime writer

He is a shallow, affected, self-conscious fribble.
Vita Sackville-West, English author, poet and
gardener, on Max Beerbohm, English writer and critic

Waldo is one of those people who would be enor-
mously improved by death.
Saki (H. H. Munro), English short story writer, on
Ralph Waldo Emerson, American essayist and poet

A totally disinherited waif.
George Santayana, Spanish-born philosopher, author
and poet, on Charles Dickens, English novelist

I have read several fragments of *Ulysses* in its serial form. It is a revolting record of a disgusting phase of civilisation; but it is a truthful one; and I should like to put a cordon around Dublin; round up every male person in it between the ages of fifteen and thirty; force them to read it; and ask them whether on reflection they could see anything amusing in all that foul mouthed, foul minded derision and obscenity.

> George Bernard Shaw, Irish playwright, on James
> Joyce, Irish novelist and poet, 1921

I could not write the words Mr Joyce uses: my prudish hands would refuse to form the letters.

> George Bernard Shaw, on James Joyce

Living almost always among intellectuals, she preserved to the age of fifty-six that contempt for ideas which is normal among girls and boys of fifteen.

> Odell Shepard, American poet, professor and politi-
> cian, on Louisa May Alcott, American novelist

Mr Lawrence looked like a plaster gnome on a stone toadstool in some suburban garden. He looked as if he had just returned from spending an uncomfortable night in a very dark cave.

> Dame Edith Sitwell, English poet and critic, on D. H.
> Lawrence, English novelist, poet and playwright

Virginia Woolf's writing is no more than glamorous knitting. I believe she must have a pattern somewhere.
  Dame Edith Sitwell, on Virginia Woolf, English
  novelist

I enjoyed talking to her, but thought nothing of her writing. I considered her a beautiful little knitter.
  Dame Edith Sitwell, on Virginia Woolf

He has occasional flashes of silence that make his conversation perfectly delightful.
  Sydney Smith, English wit and clergyman, on Thomas
  Babington Macaulay, English historian and politician

A village explainer. Excellent if you were a village, but if you were not, not.
  Gertrude Stein, American novelist and poet, on Ezra
  Pound, American poet and critic

Like a large shaggy dog, just unchained, scouring the beaches of the world and baying at the moon.
  Robert Louis Stevenson, Scottish novelist, on Walt
  Whitman, American writer

An essentially private man, who wished his total indifference to public notice to be universally recognised.
  Tom Stoppard, English playwright, on James Joyce,
  Irish novelist and poet

Personally I would rather have written *Winnie-the-Pooh* than the collected works of Brecht.
  Tom Stoppard, 1972

He is a mediocre man – and knows it, or suspects it, which is worse; he will come to no good, and in the meantime he's treated rudely by waiters and is not really admired even by the middle-class dowagers.
  Lytton Strachey, English writer and critic, on E. M.
  Forster, English novelist

He has the most remarkable and seductive genius – and I should say about the smallest in the world.
  Lytton Strachey, on Max Beerbohm, English writer
  and critic

The verses, when they were written, resembled nothing so much as spoonfuls of boiling oil, ladled out by a fiendish monkey at an upstairs window upon such of the passers-by whom the wretch had a grudge against.
  Lytton Strachey, on Alexander Pope, English satirical
  poet and translator

Then Edith Sitwell appeared, her nose longer than an ant-eater's, and read some of her absurd stuff.
  Lytton Strachey, on Dame Edith Sitwell

Steele might become a reasonably good writer if he would pay a little attention to grammar, learn something about the propriety and disposition of words and, incidentally, get some information on the subject he intends to handle.

    Jonathan Swift, Anglo-Irish satirist and poet, on
    Richard Steele, Irish writer and politician

Carlyle is a poet to whom nature has denied the faculty of verse.

    Alfred, Lord Tennyson, former British Poet Laureate,
    on Thomas Carlyle, Scottish philosopher, essayist
    and historian

Reading him is like wading through glue.

    Alfred, Lord Tennyson, on Ben Jonson, English poet,
    playwright and critic

Mr Kipling ... stands for everything in this cankered world which I would wish were otherwise.

    Dylan Thomas, Welsh poet and writer, on Rudyard
    Kipling, English poet and writer

Open him at any page: and there lies the English language not, as George Moore said of Pater, in a glass coffin, but in a large, sultry and unhygienic box.

    Dylan Thomas, on William Wordsworth, English
    Romantic poet

Isn't she a poisonous thing of a woman, lying, conceal-ing, flipping, plagiarising, misquoting and being as clever a literary publicist as ever?

    Dylan Thomas, on Dame Edith Sitwell

Walt Whitman was not only eager to talk about himself but reluctant to have the conversation stray from the subject for too long.

    Henry David Thoreau, American author and natural-
    ist, on the American writer

You talk about yourself a great deal. That's why there are no distinctive characters in your writing. Your characters are all alike. You probably don't under-stand women; you've never depicted one successfully.

    Leo Tolstoy, Russian writer, to Maxim Gorky,
    Russian writer and activist

I have read – nay, I have bought! – Carlyle's *Latter Day Pamphlets*, and look on my eight shillings as very much thrown away. To me it appears that the grain of sense is so smothered up in a sack of the sheerest trash, that the former is valueless … I look on him as a man who was always in danger of going mad in literature and who has now done so.

    Anthony Trollope, English novelist, on Thomas Carlyle

Also, to be fair, there is another word of praise due to this ship's library: it contains no copy of *The Vicar of Wakefield*, that strange menagerie of complacent hypocrites and idiots, of theatrical cheap-john heroes and heroines, who are always showing off, of bad people who are not interesting, and good people who are fatiguing.

Mark Twain, American author and humorist, on Oliver Goldsmith, Anglo-Irish novelist, poet and playwright

Then comes Sir Walter Scott with his enchantments, and by his single might checks ... progress, and even turns it back; sets the world in love with dreams and phantoms; with decayed and swinish forms of religion; with decayed and degraded systems of government; with the silliness and emptiness, sham grandeurs, sham gauds, and sham chivalries of a brainless and worthless long-vanished society. He did measureless harm; more real and lasting harm, perhaps, than any other individual that ever wrote.

Mark Twain, on Sir Walter Scott, Scottish historical novelist

Harte is a liar, a thief, a swindler, a snob, a sot, a sponge, a coward, a Jeremy Diddler, he is brim full of treachery, and he conceals his Jewish birth as carefully as if he considered it a disgrace. How do I know? By the best of all evidence, personal observation.

Mark Twain, on Bret Harte, American author and poet

He is a bad novelist and a fool. The combination usually makes for great popularity in the US.
> Gore Vidal, American critic and commentator, on Alexander Solzhenitsyn, Russian novelist

In her last days she resembled a spoiled pear.
> Gore Vidal, on Gertrude Stein

I can't stand him. Nobody will think to ask because I'm supposedly jealous; but I out-sell him. I'm more popular than he is, and I don't take him very seriously … oh, he comes on like the worker's son, like a modern-day D. H. Lawrence, but he's just another boring little middle-class boy hustling his way to the top if he can do it.
> Gore Vidal, on John Updike, American novelist

He's a full-fledged housewife from Kansas with all the prejudices.
> Gore Vidal, on Truman Capote, American writer and journalist

It is inhuman to attack Capote. You are attacking an elf.
> Gore Vidal, on Truman Capote

It was a good career move.
> Gore Vidal, on the death of Truman Capote

If its length be not considered a merit, it hath no other.
  Edmund Waller, English poet and politician, on John
  Milton's *Paradise Lost*

Like eating haggis, reading Dick Francis is something
that must be done once but never again.
  Guy Walters, British historian and journalist, on the
  British crime writer

… a mercenary, hypochondriacal flibbertigibbet who
doesn't take in one of the six words addressed to him.
  Evelyn Waugh, English novelist, on Beverly Nicholls,
  English author, playwright and journalist

One could always baffle Conrad by saying 'humour'.
It was one of our damned English tricks he had never
learned to tackle.
  H. G. Wells, English novelist, historian and commentator, on Joseph Conrad, Polish author

With a pig's eyes that never look up, with a pig's snout
that loves muck, with a pig's brain that knows only the
sty, and a pig's squeal that cries only when he is hurt,
he sometimes opens his pig's mouth, tusked and ugly,
and lets out the voice of God, railing at the whitewash
that covers the manure about his habitat.
  William Allen White, American editor, writer and
  politician, on H. L. Mencken, American humorist,
  1928

A reptile marking his path wherever he goes and breathing a mildew at everything fresh and fragrant; a midnight ghoul preying on rottenness and repulsive filth. A creature hated by his nearest intimates and bearing his consciousness thereof upon his distorted features and upon his despicable soul.

> Walt Whitman, American writer, on James Gordon
> Bennett, American editor and journalist

Tell me, when you're alone with Max, does he take off his face and reveal his mask?

> Oscar Wilde, Irish writer, essayist and playwright, on
> English writer Max Beerbohm

He hunts down the obvious with the enthusiasm of a short-sighted detective.

> Oscar Wilde, on James Payne, writer

George Moore wrote excellent English until he discovered grammar.

> Oscar Wilde, on the Irish poet and novelist

As a writer he has mastered everything except language: he can do everything except tell a story: as an artist he is everything except articulate.

> Oscar Wilde, on George Meredith, English novelist
> and poet

There are two ways of disliking poetry: one way is to dislike it, the other is to read Pope.
  Oscar Wilde, on Alexander Pope, English satirical
  poet and translator

I always said that Truman had a voice so high it could only be detected by bats.
  Tennessee Williams, American playwright, on Truman
  Capote

His style has the desperate jauntiness of an orchestra fiddling away for dear life on a sinking ship.
  Edmund Wilson, American writer, critic and man of
  letters, on Evelyn Waugh

He is not a proper person to be admitted into respectable society, being the most perverse and malevolent creature that ill-luck has thrown my way.
  William Wordsworth, English Romantic poet, on
  William Hazlitt, British essayist

#LITERATURE

You should take a look at my bookshelves. I've got the complete works of Shakespeare, Whitman, Proust, Longfellow and Jane Austen.
  And I've also got some books for reading.
  Anon.

This was another of our fears: that Life wouldn't turn out to be like Literature.
   Julian Barnes, *The Sense of an Ending* (2011)

GEORGE: Books are on their way out, nowadays, didn't you know that? Words are on their last legs. Words, print and also thought. That's also for the high jump. The sentence, that dignified entity with subject and predicate, is shortly to be made illegal. Wherever two or three words are gathered together, you see, there is a grave danger that thought might be present. All assemblies of words will be forbidden, in favour of patterns of light, videotape, every man his own telecine.
   Alan Bennett, *Getting On* (1971)

Literature exists so that where one man has lived finely, ten thousand may afterwards live finely.
   Arnold Bennett, English author and journalist

Literature is always a good card to play for honours. It makes people think that Cabinet ministers are educated.
   Arnold Bennett

Literature is mostly about having sex and not much about having children. Life is the other way round.
   David Lodge, *The British Museum is Falling Down* (1965)

In literature as in love, we are astonished at what is chosen by others.
   André Maurois, French writer

The difference between literature and journalism is that journalism is unreadable and literature is not read.

Oscar Wilde, 'The Critic as Artist' (1890)

I hate vulgar realism in literature. The man who would call a spade a spade should be compelled to use one. It is the only thing he is fit for.

Oscar Wilde, *The Picture of Dorian Gray* (1891)

Literature is the orchestration of platitudes.

Thornton Wilder, American playwright and novelist

See also #BOOKS

M

#MEMOIRS

See #AUTOBIOGRAPHY, #BIOGRAPHY

#MONEY

A large income is the best recipe for happiness I ever heard of.
  Jane Austen, English novelist

It is very difficult for the prosperous to be humble.
  Jane Austen

The freelance writer is a man who is paid per piece or per word or perhaps.
  Robert Benchley, American humorist

I should like to see a custom introduced of readers who are pleased with a book sending the author some small cash token: anything between half-a-crown and a hundred pounds. Not more than a hundred pounds

– that would be bad for my character – not less than half-a-crown – that would do no good to yours.
Cyril Connolly, English critic and writer

As a novelist, I tell stories and people give me money. Then financial planners tell me stories and I give them money.
Martin Cruz Smith, American mystery novelist

The first thing a writer has to do is find another source of income.
Ellen Gilchrist, American novelist and poet

There is no money in poetry; but then there is no poetry in money, either.
Robert Graves, English poet

J. K. Rowling's imagination was so amazing that I wanted to crawl into her head. Now, of course, I want to crawl into her bank balance.
Richard Harris, Irish actor, on acting in the *Harry Potter* films

The only sensible ends of literature are, first, the pleasurable toil of writing; second, the gratification of one's family and friends; and lastly, the solid cash.
Nathaniel Hawthorne, American novelist and short story writer

I always start a book for money. If you're married five times, you have to.
  Norman Mailer, American writer and film-maker

Poets are born, not paid.
  Wilson Mizner, American playwright and raconteur

There is only one way to make money at writing and that is to marry a publisher's daughter.
  George Orwell, *Down and Out in Paris and London* (1933)

I don't know much about being a millionaire, but I'll bet I'd be darling at it.
  Dorothy Parker, American wit

I'd like to have money. And I'd like to be a good writer. These two can come together, and I hope they will, but if that's too adorable, I'd rather have money.
  Dorothy Parker

If you want to know what God thinks of money, just look at the people he gave it to.
  Dorothy Parker

The most beautiful words in the English language are, 'Cheque enclosed.'
  Dorothy Parker

I loathe writing. On the other hand, I'm a great believer in money.

S. J. Perelman, American comic writer

Writing is the only profession where no one considers you ridiculous if you earn no money.

Jules Renard, French author

All decent people live beyond their incomes nowadays and those who aren't respectable live beyond other people's.

Saki, 'The Chronicles of Clovis' (1911)

Whenever I am asked what kind of writing is the most lucrative, I have to say, a ransom note.

H. N. Swanson, American literary agent

I never write *metropolis* for seven cents because I can get the same price for *city*. I never write *policeman* because I can get the same money for *cop*.

Mark Twain, American author and humorist

Poets, we know, are terribly sensitive people, and in my observation one of the things they are most sensitive about is money.

Robert Penn Warren, American poet, novelist and critic

N

#NEWSPAPERS

I keep reading between the lies.
  Goodman Ace, American comedy writer

He had been kicked in the head by a mule when young, and believed everything he read in the Sunday papers.
  George Ade, American writer and journalist

Instead of being arrested, as we stated, for kicking his wife down a flight of stairs and hurling a lighted kerosene lamp after her, the Rev. James P. Wellman died unmarried four years ago.
  Anon., from an American newspaper, quoted by Sir
  Edward Burne-Jones in a letter to Lady Horner

The American reading his Sunday paper in a state of lazy collapse is perhaps the most perfect symbol of the triumph of quantity over quality ... Whole forests are ground into pulp to minister to our triviality.
  Irving Babbit, American academic and literary critic

Give someone half a page in a newspaper and they think they own the world.

Jeffrey Barnard, British columnist

I read the newspaper avidly. It is my one form of continuous fiction.

Aneurin Bevan, British Labour politician

Rage is the only quality which has kept me, or anybody I have ever studied, writing columns for newspapers.

Jimmy Breslin, New York columnist

I love the weight of American Sunday newspapers. Pulling them up off the floor is good for the figure.

Noël Coward, English playwright and entertainer

I'm the Clergyman who's never been to London,
I'm the Clergyman who's never been to Town,
An enterprising journalist approached me
And every word I said he jotted down,
I had to face a battery of cameras
And hold an extra service in the snow
And all because I've *never* been to London
And haven't got the *least* desire to go!

Noël Coward, 'The Hall of Fame', *Words and Music* (1932)

Except for the Flood, nothing was ever as bad as reported.

Edgar Watson Howe, American novelist and magazine editor

When I say 'start' let's have five seconds of silence. *(Pause)* That's pretty good. That gives something for the news media to quote with absolute accuracy.

    Bobby Knight, Indiana basketball coach, 1982

Everything you read in the newspapers is absolutely true except for the rare story of which you happen to have first-hand knowledge.

    Erwin Knoll, American editor and journalist

People everywhere confuse
What they read in newspapers with news.

    A. J. Liebling, *New Yorker* journalist, 1956

You should always believe all you read in the newspapers, as this makes them more interesting.

    Rose Macaulay, *A Casual Commentary* (1925)

Once a newspaper touches a story, the facts are lost forever, even to the protagonists.

    Norman Mailer, American writer and film-maker

The indispensable requirement for a good newspaper – as eager to tell a lie as the truth.

    Norman Mailer

All successful newspapers are ceaselessly querulous and bellicose. They never defend anyone or anything if they can help it; if the job is forced on them, they tackle it by denouncing someone or something else.

    H. L. Mencken, American humorist

Any man with ambition, integrity – and $10,000,000 – can start a daily newspaper.
> Henry Morgan, 1950

Early in life I had noticed that no event is ever correctly reported in a newspaper.
> George Orwell, *Collected Essays, Journalism and Letters* (1968), ed. by Sonia Orwell and Ian Angus

I hope we never live to see the day when a thing is as bad as some of our newspapers make it.
> Will Rogers, American humorist, 1934

No self-respecting fish would be wrapped in a Murdoch newspaper.
> Mike Royko, American columnist

[A device] unable … to discriminate between a bicycle accident and the collapse of civilisation.
> George Bernard Shaw, Irish playwright, defining 'a newspaper'

An editor is one who separates the wheat from the chaff and prints the chaff.
> Adlai Stevenson, American Democratic politician

Junk journalism is the evidence of a society that has got at least one thing right, that there should be nobody with the power to dictate where responsible journalism begins.
> Tom Stoppard, *Night and Day* (1978)

RUTH: I'm with you on the free press. It's the news-papers I can't stand.

Tom Stoppard, *Night and Day* (1978)

Freedom of the press in Britain means freedom to print such of the proprietor's prejudices as the advertisers don't object to.

Hannen Swaffer, British journalist and critic

If you don't read the newspaper, you're uninformed. If you read the newspaper, you're mis-informed.

Mark Twain, American author and humorist

I think the *Cincinnati Enquirer* must be edited by children.

Mark Twain

'With regard to Policy, I expect you already have your own views. I never hamper my correspondents in any way. What the British public wants first, last and all the time is News. Remember that the Patriots are in the right and are going to win. *The Beast* stands by them four square. But they must win quickly. The British public has no interest in a war that drags on indecisively. A few sharp victories, some conspicu-ous acts of personal bravery on the Patriot side and a colourful entry into the capital. That is *The Beast* Policy for the war.'

Evelyn Waugh, *Scoop* (1938)

No passion in the world, no love or hate, is equal to the passion to alter someone else's copy.
H. G. Wells, English novelist, historian and commentator

The conscience of an editor is purely decorative.
Oscar Wilde, Irish writer, essayist and playwright

In the old days men had the rack, now they have the Press.
Oscar Wilde, 'The Soul of Man under Socialism' (1891)

It is useless to dangle rich bribes before our eyes. *Cosy Moments* cannot be muzzled. You doubtless mean well, according to your – if I may say so – somewhat murky lights, but we are not for sale, except at ten cents weekly. From the hills of Maine to the Everglades of Florida, from Sandy Hook to San Francisco, from Portland, Oregon, to Melonsquashville, Tennessee, one sentence is in every man's mouth. And what is that sentence? I give you three guesses. You give it up? It is this: '*Cosy Moments* cannot be muzzled!'
P. G. Wodehouse, *Psmith, Journalist* (1915)

See also #JOURNALISM

#NOVELS

I know a guy who reads mystery novels backwards. He knows who did it, but he doesn't know what he did.
Anon.

Every novel should have a beginning, a muddle and an end.

Peter De Vries, American novelist

My test of a good novel is dreading to begin the last chapter.

Thomas Helm, reader and writer

Among the many problems which beset the novelist, not the least weighty is the choice of the moment at which to begin his novel.

Vita Sackville-West, English author, poet and gardener

WAGNER: One of the things that makes novels less plausible than history, I find, is the way they shrink from coincidence.

Tom Stoppard, *Night and Day* (1978)

Most writers are not quick-witted when they talk. Novelists, in particular, drag themselves around in society like gut-shot bears.

Kurt Vonnegut, American novelist

In every first novel, the hero is the author as Christ or Faust.

Oscar Wilde, Irish writer, essayist and playwright

I quite admit that modern novels have many good points. All I insist on is that, as a class, they are quite unreadable.

Oscar Wilde, 'The Decay of Lying' (1891)

Every author really wants to have letters printed in the papers. Unable to make the grade, he drops down a rung of the ladder and writes novels.

P. G. Wodehouse, English humorist

It has been well said that an author who expects results from a first novel is in a position similar to that of a man who drops a rose petal down the Grand Canyon of Arizona and listens for the echo.

P. G. Wodehouse, *Cocktail Time* (1958)

'I write about stalwart men, strong but oh so gentle, and girls with wide grey eyes and hair the colour of ripe wheat, who are always having misunderstandings and going to Africa. The men, that is. The girls stay at home and marry the wrong bimbos. But there's a happy ending. The bimbos break their necks in the hunting field and the men come back in the last chapter and they and the girls get together in the twilight, and all around is the scent of English flowers and birds singing their evensong in the shrubbery. Makes me shudder to think of it.'

P. G. Wodehouse, *Ice in the Bedroom* (1961)

See also #BESTSELLERS, #BOOKS, #FICTION, #LITERATURE, #PROSE

O

#OBITUARIES

Dr Ramsden cannot read
The Times obituary today
He's dead.
Let monographs on silk worms
By other people be
Thrown away
Unread.
For he who best could understand and criticise them,
he
Lies clay. In bed.

> John Betjeman, English poet, obituary poem for Dr
> Walter Ramsden, 1947

We have lost our little Hanner in a very painful manner,
And we often asked, How can her harsh sufferings
be borne?
When her death was first reported, her aunt got up
and snorted
With the grief that she supported, for it made her
feel forlorn.

She was such a little seraph that her father, who is sheriff,

Really doesn't seem to care if he ne'er smiles in life again.

She has gone, we hope, to heaven, at the early age of seven

(Funeral starts off at eleven), where she'll never more have pain.

Charles Heber Clark ('Max Adeler'), 'Hanner', *Mr Slimmer's Funeral Verses for the Morning Argus*

Nothing concentrates the mind more than reading about oneself in the past tense.

Christopher Hitchens, British–American author and journalist, on reading a premature announcement of his own death in an art gallery catalogue

I want to write my own eulogy, and I want to write it in Latin. It seems only fitting to read a dead language at my funeral.

Jarod Kintz, American novelist

That would be a good thing for them to cut on my tombstone: Wherever she went, including here, it was against her better judgment.

Dorothy Parker, American wit

See also #EPITAPHS, #LAST WORDS

#OBSCENITY

Obscenity is whatever gives a judge an erection.
  Anon.

It's a heavy breather wanting to reverse the charges...
  Marc, cartoon in *The Times*, 1977

Obscenity is what happens to shock some elderly and ignorant magistrate.
  Bertrand Russell, *Look*, 1954

Obscenity can be found in every book except the telephone directory.
  George Bernard Shaw, Irish playwright

Under certain circumstances, profanity provides a relief denied even to prayer.
  Mark Twain, American author and humorist

See also #CENSORSHIP, #PORNOGRAPHY

#OXYMORONS

FIFTEEN OXYMORONS:
1. Pretty ugly
2. Act naturally
3. Advanced BASIC
4. Genuine imitation
5. Good grief

6. Working holiday
7. Almost exactly
8. Government organisation
9. Alone together
10. Business ethics
11. Military intelligence
12. Peace force
13. Charm offensive
14. Fun run
   Anon.

See also #ENGLISH LANGUAGE, THE, #WORDS

P

#PLAGIARISM

Creativity is great but plagiarism is faster.
  Anon.

Plagiarism saves time.
  Anon., on a T-shirt seen in Paris, 2013

About the most originality that any writer can hope to achieve honestly is to steal with good judgment.
  Josh Billings, American humorist

Plagiarists are always suspicious of being stolen from.
  Samuel Taylor Coleridge, English poet, critic and philosopher

Goethe said there would be little left of him if he were to discard what he owed to others.
  Charlotte Cushman, American actress

I don't like composers who think. It gets in the way of their plagiarism.

Howard Dietz, American lyricist and librettist

All my best thoughts were stolen by the ancients.

Ralph Waldo Emerson, American essayist and poet

What is originality? Undetected plagiarism.

Dean William R. Inge, English author, priest and academic

If you steal from one author, it's plagiarism; if you steal from many, its research.

Wilson Mizner, American playwright and raconteur

I'd rather be caught holding up a bank than stealing so much as a two-word phrase from another writer.

Jack Smith, American writer

It's not plagiarism – I'm recycling words, as any good environmentally conscious writer would do.

Uniek Swain, writer

Fine words! I wonder where you stole them.

Jonathan Swift, Anglo-Irish satirist and poet

Immature artists imitate. Mature artists steal.

Lionel Trilling, American author and critic

I do borrow from other writers. I can only say in my defence, like the woman brought before the judge on a charge of kleptomania, 'I do steal, but, Your Honour, only from the very best stores.'

Thornton Wilder, American playwright and novelist

#POETS AND POETRY

Never trust a poet who can drive. Never trust a poet at the wheel. If he *can* drive, distrust the poems.

Martin Amis, *The Information* (1995)

Anon., Idem, Ibid. and Trad.
Wrote much that is morally bad:
Some ballads, some shanties,
All poems on panties –
And limericks, too, one must add.

Anon.

The American constitution protects free speech, but only the American sense of humour protects free verse.

Anon.

Generally speaking, nobody knows a poet is alive until he's dead.

Anon.

There is the view that poetry should improve your life. I think people confuse it with the Salvation Army.

John Ashbery, American poet

Poetry might be defined as the clear expression of mixed feelings.
   W. H. Auden, 'New Year Letter' (1941)

I gave up on new poetry myself thirty years ago, when most of it began to read like coded messages passing between lonely aliens on a hostile world.
   Russell Baker, American writer and satirist

Elegy, *n*. A composition in verse, in which, without employing any of the methods of humor, the writer aims to produce in the reader's mind the dampest kind of dejection. The most famous English example begins somewhat like this:
   The cur foretells the knell of parting day;
   The loafing herd winds slowly o'er the lea
   The wise man homeward plods; I only stay
   To fiddle-faddle in a minor key.
   Ambrose Bierce, *The Devil's Dictionary* (1911)

If it doesn't work horizontally as prose...
it
probably
won't
work
any
better
vertically
pretending
to
be
poetry.
   Robert Brault, American poet

Longfellow is to poetry what the barrel organ is to music.
  Van Wyck Brooks, American critic and biographer, on
  American poet Henry Wadsworth Longfellow

I recently bought a book of free verse. For $12.
  George Carlin, American comedian

Why should poetry have to make sense?
  Charlie Chaplin, English comic actor

Poets have been mysteriously silent on the subject
of cheese.
  G. K. Chesterton, *Alarms and Discursions* (1910)

We invite people like that to tea, but we don't
marry them.
  Lady Chetwode, on her future son-in-law, the English
  poet John Betjeman

Poetry is indispensable – if I only knew what for.
  Jean Cocteau, French poet, novelist and dramatist

The worst tragedy for a poet is to be admired through
being misunderstood.
  Jean Cocteau

I know that poetry is indispensable, but to what I
couldn't say.
  Jean Cocteau, quoted in *The Observer*, 1955

The only really difficult thing about a poem is the critic's explanation of it.

Frank Moore Colby, American educator and writer

The phone rings and I curse. Literary editor. Seasonal verse.

Wendy Cope, English poet

I used to think all poets were Byronic – mad, bad and dangerous to know. And then I met a few. They're mostly as wicked as ginless tonic and wild as pension plans.

Wendy Cope

The reason modern poetry is difficult is so that the poet's wife cannot understand it.

Wendy Cope

We're just waiting for the moment his poetic licence expires.

Noël Coward, English playwright and entertainer, of Maxwell Anderson, American playwright and poet

A prose writer gets tired of writing prose, and wants to be a poet. So he begins every line with a capital letter, and keeps on writing prose.

Samuel McChord Crothers, Unitarian minister and essayist

I don't like to boast, but I have probably skipped more poetry than any other person of my age and weight in this country.

    Will Cuppy, American humorist and critic

The most important thing for poets to do is to write as little as possible.

    T. S. Eliot, American poet and critic

He tells you, in the sombrest notes,
If poets want to get their oats,
The first step is to slit their throats.
The way to divide
The sheep of poetry from the goats
Is suicide.

    James Fenton, 'Letter to John Fuller', *Children in Exile* (1984)

A true sonnet goes eight lines and then takes a turn for the better or worse and goes six or eight lines more.

    Robert Frost, American poet

Writing free verse is like playing tennis with the net down.

    Robert Frost, speech at Milton Academy, Mass., 1935

As soon as war is declared, it is impossible to hold the poets back.

    Jean Giraudoux, French novelist, diplomat and playwright

Little Mary from Boston, Mass.
Stepped into water up to her ankles.
It doesn't rhyme now,
But wait till the tide comes in.
> Graffito, New Haven, 1976

... I found a simple plan
Which makes the lamest lyrics scan!
When I've a syllable de trop,
I cut it off, with apol.:
This verbal sacrifice, I know,
May irritate the schol.:
But all must praise my dev'lish cunn.
Who realise that Time is Mon.
> Harry Graham, 'Poetical Economy', *Deportmental Ditties* (1909)

Every English poet should master the rules of grammar before he attempts to bend or break them.
> Robert Graves, English poet

There are poems about the Internet and about the shipping forecast but very few by women celebrating men.
> Germaine Greer, Australian academic and author, addressing the Poetry Society

Poetry books are handy implements for killing persistent irritating flies.
> Geoffrey Grigson, British critic and poet

A poet who reads his verse in public may have other nasty habits.
  Robert A. Heinlein, American science fiction writer

It's hard to say why writing verse
Should terminate in drink or worse.
  A. P. Herbert, English wit, *Punch* magazine

I could no more define poetry than a terrier can define a rat.
  A. E. Housman, English Classical scholar and poet

A poem is no place for an idea.
  Edgar Watson Howe, *Country Town Sayings* (1911)

Poet: a person born with an instinct for poverty.
  Elbert Hubbard, American writer, artist and philosopher

God and I both knew what this poem of mine meant once; now God alone knows.
  Friedrich Klopstock, German poet

When I get sent manuscripts from aspiring poets, I do one of two things: if there is no self-addressed envelope, I throw it into the bin. If there is, I write and tell them to fuck off.
  Philip Larkin, English poet

I can't understand these chaps who go round American universities explaining how they write poems. It's like going round explaining how you sleep with your wife.

Philip Larkin, quoted by John Updike in the *New York Times*, 1986

The Sitwells belong to the history of publicity rather than of poetry.

F. R. Leavis, British literary critic

If you are of the opinion that the contemplation of suicide is sufficient evidence of a poetic nature, do not forget that actions speak louder than words.

Fran Lebowitz, American author and commentator

Show me a poet and I'll show you a shit.

A. J. Liebling, *New Yorker* journalist

Indifference to poetry is one of the most conspicuous characteristics of the human race.

Robert Lynd, Irish writer and essayist

Perhaps no person can be a poet, or can even enjoy poetry, without a certain unsoundness of mind.

Thomas Babington Macaulay, English historian and politician

The only problem
with Haiku is that you just
get started and the

Roger McGough, English poet

Publishing a volume of verse is like dropping a rose petal down the Grand Canyon and waiting for the echo.
Don Marquis, American humorist

Nobody is more confident than a bad poet.
Martial, Latin poet

My favourite poem is the one that starts, 'Thirty days has September', because it actually tells you something.
Groucho Marx, actor and comedian, 1984

The crown of literature is poetry. It is its end and aim. It is the sublimest activity of the human mind. It is the achievement of beauty and delicacy. The writer of prose can only step aside when the poet passes.
W. Somerset Maugham, *Saturday Review*, 1957

A poet more than thirty years old is simply an overgrown child.
H. L. Mencken, American humorist

Arnold is a dandy Isaiah, a poet without passion whose verse, written in surplice, is for freshmen and for gentle maidens who will be wooed to the arms of these future rectors.
George Meredith, English novelist and poet, on the English poet and critic Matthew Arnold

The poetry world is very small and full of green-eyed snapping fish.

Andrew Motion, English poet, novelist and
biographer

I'd rather be a great bad poet than a bad good poet.

Ogden Nash, American poet

Perhaps the saddest lot that can befall mortal man is to be the husband of a lady poet.

George Jean Nathan, American editor and drama critic

Roses are red,
Violets are blue,
If a poem doesn't rhyme,
Some people think it's somehow superior to one that does.

Frederick Oliver, English wit

Having considered the matter in – of course – all its aspects, I have decided that there is no excuse for poetry. Poetry gives no adequate return in money, is expensive to print by reason of the waste of space occasioned by its form, and nearly always promulgates illusory concepts of life. But a better case for the banning of all poetry is the simple fact that most of it is bad. Nobody is going to manufacture a thousand tons of jam in the expectation that five tons may be eatable. Furthermore, poetry has the effect on the negligible handful who read it of stimulating them to

write poetry themselves. One poem, if widely dissemi-
nated, will breed perhaps a thousand inferior copies.

    Brian O'Nolan, writing as Myles na Gopaleen, *The
    Best of Myles na Gopaleen*, ed. by Flann O'Brien
    (1968)

I'd rather flunk my Wasserman test,
Than read the poems of Edgar Guest.

    Dorothy Parker, American wit

A poem is a form of refrigeration that stops language
going bad.

    Peter Porter, English poet

... it occurred to me that I would like to be a poet. The
chief qualification, I understand, is that you must be
born. Well, I hunted up my birth certificate, and found
that I was all right on that score.

    Saki, 'Reginald's Rubaiyat' (1904)

Poetry is the synthesis of hyacinths and biscuits.

    Carl Sandburg, American writer and editor

All poets' wives have rotten lives
Their husbands look at them like knives.

    Delmore Schwartz, American poet and short story
    writer

Poetry is like fish: if it's fresh, it's good; if it's stale, it's
bad; and if you're not certain, try it on the cat.

    Osbert Sitwell, English writer

In no other job have I ever had to deal with such utterly abnormal people. Yes, it is true, poetry does something to them.

> Muriel Spark, Scottish novelist, on working for the
> Poetry Society, 1992

A publisher of today would as soon see a burglar in his office as a poet.

> Henry de Vere Stacpoole, Irish author

Carlyle is a poet to whom nature has denied the faculty of verse.

> Alfred, Lord Tennyson, former British Poet Laureate,
> 1870

Poetry is not the most important thing in life ... I'd much rather sit in a hot bath reading Agatha Christie and sucking sweets.

> Dylan Thomas, Welsh poet, 1943

I often covered more than a hundred sheets of paper with drafts, revisions, rewritings, ravings, doodlings, and intensely concentrated work to produce a single verse.

> Dylan Thomas, 1948

I am a painstaking, conscientious, involved and devious craftsman in words ... I use everything to make my poems work and move in the directions I want them to: old tricks, new tricks, puns, portmanteauwords, paradox, allusion, paranomasia, paragam, catachresis, slang, assonantal rhymes, vowel rhymes, sprung rhythm ... Poets have got to enjoy themselves sometimes.

 Dylan Thomas, *Poetic Manifesto* (1951)

Poetry is trouble dunked in tears.

 Gwyn Thomas, Welsh poet

Poems are never finished – just abandoned.

 Paul Valéry, French poet, essayist and philosopher

Poetry is to prose as dancing is to walking.

 John Wain, English novelist, talk on BBC Radio, 1976

There are two ways of disliking poetry: one way is to dislike it, the other is to read Pope.

 Oscar Wilde, Irish writer, essayist and playwright, on
 English satirical poet and translator Alexander Pope

... a form of poetry which cannot possibly hurt anybody, even if translated into French.

 Oscar Wilde, review in the *Pall Mall Gazette*

A poet can survive everything but a misprint.

 Oscar Wilde, *Pall Mall Gazette*, 1886

All bad poetry springs from genuine feeling. To be natural is to be obvious, and to be obvious is to be inartistic.

 Oscar Wilde, 'The Critic as Artist' (1890)

We have been able to have fine poetry in England because the public do not read it, and consequently do not influence it. The public like to insult poets because they are individual, but once they have insulted them, they leave them alone.

Oscar Wilde, 'The Soul of Man under Socialism' (1891)

Peotry is sissy stuff that rhymes. Weedy people say la and fie and swoon when they see a bunch of daffodils. Aktually there is only one piece of peotry in the english language.

The Brook
i come from haunts of coot and hern
i make a sudden sally
and-er-hem-er-hem-the fern
to bicker down a valley.

Geoffrey Willans and Ronald Searle, *Down with Skool!* (1953)

Dark hair fell in a sweep over his forehead. He looked like a man who would write *vers libre*, as indeed he did.

P. G. Wodehouse, *The Girl on the Boat* (1922)

Rodney Spelvin was the sort of man who would produce a slim volume of verse bound in squashy mauve leather at the drop of a hat, mostly on the subject of sunsets and pixies.

P. G. Wodehouse, *The Heart of a Goof* (1926)

I may as well tell you that if you are going about the place thinking things pretty, you will never make a modern poet. Be poignant, man, be poignant!

P. G. Wodehouse, *The Small Bachelor* (1927)

She could never forget that the man she loved was a man with a past. He had been a poet. Deep down in her soul there was always the corroding fear lest at any moment a particularly fine sunset or the sight of a rose in bud might undo all the work she had done, sending Rodney hotfoot once more to his Thesaurus and rhyming dictionary. It was for this reason that she always hurried him indoors when the sun began to go down and refused to have rose trees in her garden.

P. G. Wodehouse, *Nothing Serious* (1950)

See also #LIMERICKS

#PORNOGRAPHY

Pornography is in the groin of the beholder.

Anon.

Many a writer would be unreadable if he didn't resort to words that are unprintable.

Anon.

I always start writing with a clean piece of paper and a dirty mind.

Patrick Dennis, American author

It is written in the stickily overwrought language of the ageing prep-school house-master who had sex once in 1987 and still can't quite believe his luck.

John Diamond, of *The Erotic Review*, *The Times*, 2000

If the purpose of pornography is to excite sexual desire, it is unnecessary for the young, inconvenient for the middle-aged and unseemly for the old.

Malcolm Muggeridge, English journalist

At last, an unprintable book that is readable.

Ezra Pound, on Henry Miller's *Tropic of Cancer*, 1934

Pornography is whatever happens to shock some elderly and ignorant magistrate.

Bertrand Russell, *Look*, 1954

Perhaps it would help ... to compose a letter ... to *The Times*:

Dear Sir,

I hope I am not a prude, but I feel compelled to lodge a protest against the ever-increasing flood of obscenity in dreams. Many of my friends have been as shocked and sickened as myself by the filth that is poured out nightly as soon as our eyes are closed. It is certainly not my idea of 'home entertainment'.

Night after night, the most disgraceful scenes of perversion and bestiality are perpetrated behind my eyelids … It is imperative that official action should be taken.

Kenneth Tynan, *The Sound of Two Hands Clapping* (1975)

See also #CENSORSHIP, #OBSCENITY

#PROCRASTINATION

If it weren't for the last minute, I wouldn't get anything done.

Anon.

It is an undoubted truth, that the less one has to do, the less time one finds to do it in.

Earl of Chesterfield, British statesman and man of letters

Procrastinate now, don't put it off.

Ellen DeGeneres, comedian and talk-show host

It was such a lovely day, I thought it was a pity to get up.

W. Somerset Maugham, *Our Betters* (1917)

If you want to make an easy job seem mighty hard, just keep putting off doing it.

Olin Miller, wit

If a thing's worth doing, it's worth doing late.
    Frederick Oliver, English wit

Only Robinson Crusoe had everything done by Friday.
    Sally Poplin, English writer

Never put off until tomorrow what you can do the day after tomorrow.
    Mark Twain, American author and humorist

Procrastination is something best put off until tomorrow.
    Gerald Vaughan, humorist

#PRONUNCIATION

Q: What word is always pronounced wrong?
A: 'Wrong.'
    The Big Book of Jokes and Riddles (1978)

If anyone corrects your pronunciation of a word in a public place, you have every right to punch him on the nose.
    Heywood Broun, American writer

Whose cruel idea was it for the word 'lisp' to have an 's' in it?
    George Carlin, American comedian

Aitches don't make artists – there ain't no 'H' in 'Art'.
  Albert Chevalier, 'The Cockney Trajedian', music-hall
  song

Everybody has a right to pronounce foreign names as
he chooses.
  Sir Winston Churchill, British Prime Minister
  1940–45, 1951–5

Dear Miss Manners, When is a *vase* a *vahz*?
Gentle Reader, When it is filled with *dah-zies*.
  Judith Martin, aka Miss Manners, American journalist,
  author and etiquette authority

They spell it Vinci and pronounce it Vinchy; foreigners
always spell better than they pronounce.
  Mark Twain, *The Innocent Abroad* (1869)

#PROSE

Prose is when all of the lines except the last one go on
to the end of the page. Poetry is when some of them
fall short of it.
  Matthew Arnold, British poet

For more than forty years I have been speaking prose
without knowing.
  Michel de Montaigne, French essayist

See also #FICTION, #NOVELS

#PSEUDONYMS

I wrote a book under a pen name: Bic.
　Buzz Nutley, comedian and writer

#PUBLISHERS

A publisher lives by what he feels. Authors do too, but authors are blind moles working their solitary way along their individual tunnels; the publisher is like the Pied Piper of Hamelin, piping his way along a path he wants them to follow.
　Anonymous Canadian writer and publisher

In a profession like publishing where simple accountancy is preferable to a degree in English, illiteracy is not considered to be a great drawback.
　Dominic Behan, Irish writer

Gentlemen, I agree with you that Napoleon is a tyrant, a monster, the sworn foe of our nation, and if you will, of the whole human race. But, gentlemen, we must not forget that he once shot a publisher.
　Thomas Campbell, Scottish poet

As repressed sadists are said to become policemen or butchers, so those with an irrational fear of life become publishers.
　Cyril Connolly, *Enemies of Promise* (1938)

Never buy an editor or publisher a lunch or a drink until he has bought an article, story or book from you. This rule is absolute and may be broken only at your peril.
  John Creasey, English novelist

It circulated for five years through the halls of fifteen publishers, and finally ended up with Vanguard Press which, as you can see, is rather deep into the alphabet.
  Patrick Dennis, American author

It is with publishers as with wives: one always wants somebody else's.
  Norman Douglas, English novelist

The way British publishing works is that you go from not being published no matter how good you are, to being published no matter how bad you are.
  Tibor Fischer, British novelist and short story writer

Seventeen publishers rejected the manuscript, at which time we knew we had something pretty hot.
  Kinky Friedman, American songwriter and author

No author is a man of genius to his publisher.
  Heinrich Heine, German journalist and poet

A new firm of publishers has written to me proposing to publish 'the successor' of *A Shropshire Lad*. But as they don't also offer to write it, I have to put them off.
  A. E. Housman, English Classical scholar and poet

Literature is an occupation in which you have to keep proving your talent to people who have none.

Jules Renard, French author

I don't believe in publishers who wish to butter their bannocks on both sides while they'll hardly allow an author to smell treacle. I consider they are too grabby altogether and like Methodists they love to keep the Sabbath and everything else they can lay their hands on.

Amanda Ros, Irish novelist, 1936

I object to publishers: the one service they have done me is to teach me to do without them. They combine commercial rascality with artistic touchiness and pettiness, without being either good business men or fine judges of literature. All that is necessary in the production of a book is an author and a bookseller, without any intermediate parasite.

George Bernard Shaw, Irish playwright, letter, 1895

I asked my publisher what would happen if he sold all the copies of my book he had printed. He said, 'I'll just print another ten.'

Eric Sykes, English comedian

The advance for a book should be at least as much as the cost of the lunch at which it was discussed. When I proposed this formula to an editor, he told me it was unrealistic.

Calvin Trillin, American journalist and poet

All a publisher has to do is write cheques at intervals, while a lot of deserving and industrious chappies rally round and do the real work.

P. G. Wodehouse, *My Man Jeeves* (1919)

See also #AGENTS

#PUNCTUATION

The Hitchhiker's Guide to the Galaxy skips lightly over this tangle of academic abstraction, pausing only to note that the term 'Future Perfect' has been abandoned since it was discovered not to be.

Douglas Adams, *The Restaurant at the End of the Universe* (1980)

If you take hyphens seriously, you will surely go mad.

Anon.

She was the only person I ever met who used semicolons in her love letters.

Anon.

I've had great fun doing some stories by phone with certain magazine editors … Bargaining goes on horse-trading, 'You can have the dash if I can have the semicolon.'

Margaret Atwood, interview, 1990

He's a fastidious journalist. He once telephoned a semicolon from Moscow.

James Bone, British editor and journalist

Cut out all those exclamation marks. An exclamation mark is like laughing at your own joke.

F. Scott Fitzgerald, quoted in the film *Beloved Infidel* (1959)

And if you want to know why great editors scare the pants off of writers everywhere, read *Eats, Shoots & Leaves* by Lynne Truss. The punctuation police are everywhere!

Dorothea Benton Frank, American author and biographer

A man who can put an apostrophe in the wrong place is capable of anything.

Con Houlihan, Irish journalist

I'm tired of wasting letters when punctuation will do, period.

Steve Martin, American actor and comedian

Five exclamation marks, the sure sign of an insane mind.

Terry Pratchett, *Reaper Man* (1991)

Sometimes you get a glimpse of a semicolon coming, a few lines farther on, and it is like climbing a steep path through woods and seeing a wooden bench just at a bend in the road ahead, a place where you can expect to sit for a moment, catching your breath.

> Lewis Thomas, American poet and educator

The word 'I'll' should not be divided so that the 'I' is on one line and the 'll' is on the next. The reader's attention, after the breaking up of the 'I'll', can never be successfully recaptured.

> James Thurber, American comic writer

What the semicolon's anxious supporters fret about is the tendency of contemporary writers to use a dash instead of a semicolon and thus precipitate the end of the world. Are they being alarmist?

> Lynne Truss, *Eats, Shoots & Leaves: The Zero Tolerance Approach to Punctuation* (2003)

Punctuation marks are the traffic signals of language: they tell us to slow down, notice this, take a detour, and stop.

> Lynne Truss, *Eats, Shoots & Leaves: The Zero Tolerance Approach to Punctuation* (2003)

The rule is: don't use commas like a stupid person. I mean it.

> Lynne Truss, *Eats, Shoots & Leaves: The Zero Tolerance Approach to Punctuation* (2003)

Cast iron rules will not answer ... what is one man's colon is another man's comma.
  Mark Twain, American author and humorist

Commas in the *New Yorker* fall with the precision of knives in a circus act, outlining the victim.
  E. B. White, American author and *New Yorker* contributor

'Sir Jasper Finch-Farrowmere?' said Wilfred. 'ffinch-ffarrowmere,' corrected the visitor, his sensitive ear detecting the capitals.
  P. G. Wodehouse, *Meet Mr Mulliner* (1928)

#PUNS

A pun is a short quip followed by a long groan.
  Anon.

There was a man who entered a pun contest. He sent in ten different puns in the hope that just one of them might win.
  Sadly, no pun in ten did.
  Anon.

The inveterate punster follows a conversation as a shark follows a ship.
  Stephen Leacock, Canadian humorist

A pun is the lowest form of humor – when you don't think of it first.

Oscar Levant, American composer, author and actor

What's the difference between a joist and a girder? The first wrote *Ulysses* and the second wrote *Faust*.

Sally Poplin, English writer

Q

#QUOTATIONS

It is unbecoming for young men to utter maxims.
  Aristotle, Greek philosopher

Quotation: something that somebody said that seemed to make sense at the time.
  Egon J. Beaudoin, American wit

The surest way to make a monkey out of a man is to quote him.
  Robert Benchley, American humorist

I didn't really say everything I said.
  Yogi Berra, American baseball catcher and manager

Quoting – the act of repeating erroneously the words of another.
  Ambrose Bierce, *The Devil's Dictionary* (1911)

Next to being witty yourself, the best thing is to quote another's wit.

Christian N. Bovee, New York writer

A good conversationalist is not one who remembers what was said, but says what someone wants to remember.

John Mason Brown, American author and drama critic

People will accept your ideas much more readily if you tell them Benjamin Franklin said it first.

David H. Comins, writer

The point of quotations is that one can use another's words to be insulting.

Amanda Cross, American writer of popular mystery novels

I'm bringing out a book for the building trade. It's called *The Dictionary of Ludicrous Quotations*.

Barry Cryer, British writer and performer

When a thing has been said and well, have no scruple. Take it and copy it.

Anatole France, French poet, journalist and novelist

She had a pretty gift for quotation, which is a serviceable substitute for wit...

W. Somerset Maugham, *The Creative Impulse* (1926)

My favourite quotation is £8.10 for a second-hand suit.
  Spike Milligan, English writer and comedian

I quote others only to better express myself.
  Michel de Montaigne, *The Complete Essays*

The next best thing to being clever is being able to quote someone who is.
  Mary Pettibone Poole, *A Glass Eye at a Keyhole* (1938)

The trouble with words is that you never know whose mouths they've been in.
  Dennis Potter, English screenwriter and journalist

Quotes are just fancy ways of stating the obvious.
  Gerald Prunty, Scottish writer, *Sleepfighting*

A fine quotation is a diamond on the finger of a man of wit, and a pebble in the hand of a fool.
  Joseph Roux, French poet, priest and philologist

Almost every wise saying has an opposite one, no less wise, to balance it.
  George Santayana, *The Life of Reason* (1906)

I always have a quotation for everything – it saves original thinking.
  Dorothy L. Sayers, *Have His Carcase* (1932)

I shall never be ashamed of citing a bad author if the line is good.
  Seneca, Roman philosopher

I often quote myself. It adds spice to my conversation.
George Bernard Shaw, Irish playwright

To be occasionally quoted is the only fame I care for.
Alexander Smith, *Dreamthorp* (1863)

It's better to be quotable than to be honest.
Tom Stoppard, *The Guardian*, 1973

In the dying world I come from, quotation is a national vice.
Evelyn Waugh, English novelist

Everything of importance has been said before by somebody who did not discover it.
Alfred North Whitehead, English mathematician and philosopher

I don't know if you happen to be familiar with a poem called 'The Charge of the Light Brigade' by the bird Tennyson whom Jeeves had mentioned when speaking of the fellow whose strength was as the strength of ten … the thing goes, as you probably know,
Tum tiddle umpty-pum
Tum tiddle umpty-pum
Tum tiddle umpty-pum
and this brought you to the snapperoo or pay-off which was 'someone had blundered'.
P. G. Wodehouse, *Jeeves and the Feudal Spirit* (1954)

See also #EPIGRAMS, #REFERENCE

R

#READING AND READERS

I do a lot of reading about serial killers, mostly *How To* books.
Roseanne Barr, American actress and comedian

Nearly all bookish people are snobs and especially the more enlightened among them. They are apt to assume that if a writer has immense circulation, if he is enjoyed by plain persons, and if he can fill several theatres at once, he cannot possibly be worth reading and merits only indifference and disdain.
Arnold Bennett, English author and journalist, 1928

I'm dyslexic. There was a sign outside my school that said, 'Slow Children' which didn't do much for our self-esteem. Then again, we couldn't read it.
Jimmy Carr, British comedian

Finally, from so little sleeping and so much reading, his brain dried up and he went completely out of his mind.
Miguel de Cervantes Saavedra, *Don Quixote* (1605)

I can't write without a reader. It's precisely like a kiss – you can't do it alone.

John Cheever, American novelist

The mere brute pleasure of reading – the sort of pleasure a cow must have in grazing.

Lord Chesterfield, British statesman and man of letters

The human race, to which so many of my readers belong...

G. K. Chesterton, *The Napoleon of Notting Hill* (1904)

Having to read footnotes resembles having to go downstairs to answer the door while in the midst of making love.

Noël Coward, English playwright and entertainer

There are times when I think that the reading I have done in the past has had no effect except to cloud my mind and make me indecisive.

Robertson Davies, Canadian writer and critic

I honestly believe there is absolutely nothing like going to bed with a good book. Or a friend who's read one.

Phyllis Diller, American actress and comedian

An author who talks about his own books is almost as bad as a mother who talks about her own children.

Benjamin Disraeli, British Prime Minister 1868, 1874–80

When I want to read a book, I write one.
> Benjamin Disraeli

Reading, after a certain age, diverts the mind too much from its creative pursuits. Any man who reads too much and uses his own brain too little falls into lazy habits of thinking.
> Albert Einstein, German-born theoretical physicist

I always read the last page of a book first, so that, if I die before I finish, I will know how it turned out.
> Nora Ephron, American novelist and screenwriter

Whenever you read a good book, it's like the author is right there, in the room talking to you. Which is why I don't like to read good books.
> Jack Handy, American comedy writer

People in general do not willingly read if they have anything else to amuse them.
> Samuel Johnson, English poet, biographer and
> lexicographer

No person who can read is ever successful at cleaning out an attic.
> Ann Landers, American advice columnist

Everyone probably thinks that I'm a raving nympho-maniac, that I have an insatiable sexual appetite, when the truth is, I'd rather read a book.
> Madonna, interview, 1991

The chief knowledge that a man gets from reading books is the knowledge that very few of them are worth reading.
  H. L. Mencken, American humorist

I have only read one book in my life and that is *White Fang*. It's so frightfully good that I've never bothered to read another.
  Nancy Mitford, novelist and biographer

She'd stopped reading the kind of women's magazine that talked about romance and knitting and started reading the kind of women's magazine that talked about orgasms ... making a mental note to have one if ever the occasion presented itself.
  Terry Pratchett, English writer

When you come to the end of a crime novel, something at least in this huge, chaotic world has been settled.
  J. B. Priestley, English novelist, playwright and broad-
  caster, quoted in the *Manchester Guardian/Weekly*

There are two motives for reading a book; one, that you enjoy it; the other, that you can boast about it.
  Bertrand Russell, Welsh philosopher and social critic

I've never known any trouble that an hour's reading didn't assuage.
  Charles de Secondat, French social commentator and
  political thinker

Never read a book and you will become a rich man.
  Timothy Shelley, English aristocrat

It's not easy having dyslexia. Last week I went to a toga party as a goat.
  Arthur Smith, English comedian

This nice and subtle happiness of reading, this joy not chilled by age, this polite and unpunished vice, this selfish, serene, life-long intoxication.
  Logan Pearsall Smith, American essayist and critic

Why pay a dollar for a bookmark? Use the dollar as a bookmark.
  Fred Stoller, stand-up comedian, actor, writer

If you are in difficulties with a book, try the element of surprise; attack it at an hour when it isn't expecting it.
  H. G. Wells, English novelist, historian and
  commentator

I just got out of the hospital. I was in a speed-reading accident. I hit a bookmark.
  Steven Wright, American comedian

See also #BOOKS, #LIBRARIES

#REFERENCE

Circular Definition. See Definition, Circular.
  Anon.

How come there's no other name for thesaurus?
  Anon.

Is there another word for synonym?
  Anon.

An encyclopaedia is a system for collecting dust in alphabetical order.
  Mike Barfield, English writer, cartoonist, poet

MOTHER: Bobby's teacher says he ought to have an encyclopaedia.
FATHER: Let him walk to school like I had to.
  Gyles Brandreth, *1,000 Jokes: The Greatest Joke Book Ever Known* (1980)

Words fascinate me, they always have. For me, browsing in a dictionary is like being turned loose in a bank.
  Eddie Cantor, American comedian and dancer

What a comfort a dictionary is!
  Lewis Carroll, *Sylvie and Bruno Concluded* (1893)

I was in a second-hand book shop the other day and I found a book called How to Hug. I assumed it was some sort of romantic how-to book, but when I got it home, I discovered that it was volume six of the *Encyclopedia Britannica*.
  Jerry Dennis, English comedian

A synonym is a word you use when you can't spell the other one.

> Baltasar Gracián, Spanish Jesuit, writer and
> philosopher

Any word you have to hunt for in a thesaurus is the wrong word. There are no exceptions to this rule.

> Stephen King, American novelist

Words are like leaves and where they most abound
Much fruit of sense beneath is rarely found.

> Alexander Pope, 'An Essay on Criticism' (1711)

You could always tell by his conversation which volume of the *Encyclopaedia Britannica* he'd been reading. One day it would be the Alps, Andes and Apennines and the next it would be the Himalayas and the Hippocratic Oath.

> Bertrand Russell, Welsh philosopher and social critic,
> on Aldous Huxley, English writer

There is a new dictionary for masochists. It lists all the words but not in alphabetical order.

> Frank Tyger, English columnist and editorial
> cartoonist

Should not the Society of Indexers be known as Indexers, Society of, The?

> Keith Waterhouse, English columnist, *Daily Mail*

I've just been reading the dictionary. It turns out the zebra did it.

  Steven Wright, American comedian

I was reading the dictionary. I thought it was a poem about everything.

  Steven Wright

#RIDDLES

Q: What has four wheels and flies?
A: A garbage truck.

  Anon.

Q: What has sixteen legs, fourteen testicles and two tiny breasts?
A: Snow White and the Seven Dwarfs.

  Anon.

Q: What's grey, has four legs and a trunk?
A: A mouse going on holiday.

  Anon.

Q: What's green and pecks on trees?
A: Woody Wood Pickle.

  The Big Book of Jokes and Riddles (1978)

Q: What happens when the human body is completely submerged in water?
A: The telephone rings.

The Big Book of Jokes and Riddles (1978)

Q: What's worse than an octopus with tennis elbow?
A: A centipede with athlete's foot.

The Big Book of Jokes and Riddles (1978)

GEORGE: What is it that sings and has four legs?
GRACIE: Two canaries.

George Burns and Gracie Allen, *The Robert Burns Panatela Program*, CBS Radio, 1932

S

#SATIRE

The purpose of satire is to strip off the veneer of comforting allusion and cosy half-truth. And our business, as I see it, is to put it back again.
 Michael Flanders, English humorist

Satire died the day they gave Henry Kissinger the Nobel Peace Prize.
 Tom Lehrer, quoted in 'How to Survive Reagan' by
 Molly Ivins, *The Progressive*, 1986

A satirist is a man who discovers unpleasant things about himself and then says them about other people.
 Peter McArthur, English wit

Ridicule is the only honourable weapon we have left.
 Muriel Spark, 'The Desegregation of Art', *Critical Essays on Muriel Spark* (1992)

See also #HUMOUR

#SHAKESPEARE
1564–1616, English poet and playwright

I have always derived great comfort from William Shakespeare. After a depressing visit to the mirror or an unkind word from a girlfriend or an incredulous stare in the street, I say to myself: 'Well. Shakespeare looked like shit.' It works wonders.

Martin Amis, *Money* (1984)

Hamlet's Cat's Soliloquy
To go outside, and there perchance to stay
Or to remain within: that is the question:
Whether 'tis better for a cat to suffer
The cuffs and buffets of inclement weather
That Nature rains on those who roam abroad,
Or take a nap upon a scrap of carpet,
And so by dozing melt the solid hours
That clog the clock's bright gears with sullen time
And stall the dinner bell. To sit, to stare
Outdoors, and by a stare to seem to state
A wish to venture forth without delay,
Then when the portal's opened up, to stand
As if transfixed by doubt. To prowl; to sleep;
Imagine anybody having lived forty-five or fifty years without knowing Hamlet! One might as well spend one's life in a coal mine.

Hector Berlioz, composer, *Life and Letters of Berlioz*

It is difficult to restrain admirers of Shakespeare once they have begun to speak of him.
Karen Blixen, Danish author

No one yet has managed to be post-Shakespearean.
Harold Bloom, American literary critic

And now to sleep, to dream ... perchance to fart.
Anthony Bourdain, American chef

I have tried lately to read Shakespeare, and found it so intolerably dull that it nauseated me.
Charles Darwin, English naturalist

A bad experience of Shakespeare is like a bad oyster – it puts you off for life.
Judi Dench, English actress

The remarkable thing about Shakespeare is that he really is very good, in spite of all the people who say he is very good.
Robert Graves, English poet, 1964

I heard someone tried the monkeys-on-typewriters bit trying for the plays of W. Shakespeare, but all they got was the collected works of Francis Bacon.
Bill Hirst, American scientist

England has two books, the Bible and Shakespeare. England made Shakespeare, but the Bible made England.
Victor Hugo, French novelist and poet

Oh how Shakespeare would have loved cinema!
  Derek Jarman, English film director

Shakespeare opens a mine which contains gold and diamonds in unexhaustible plenty, though clouded by incrustations, debased by impurities, and mingled with a mass of meaner minerals.
  Samuel Johnson, *Samuel Johnson on Shakespeare* (c.1765)

If Shakespeare required a word and had not met it in civilised discourse, he unhesitatingly made it up.
  Amy Koppelman, American novelist

When I read Shakespeare I am struck with wonder that such trivial people should muse and thunder in such lovely language.
  D. H. Lawrence, English novelist, poet and playwright

After all, all he did was string together a lot of old, well-known quotations.
  H. L. Mencken, American humorist, on Shakespeare

The basis of all Bernard Shaw's attacks on Shakespeare is really the charge – quite true of course – that Shakespeare wasn't an enlightened member of the Fabian Society.
  George Orwell, *The Listener*, 1942

To the King's theatre, where we saw *A Midsummer Night's Dream*, which I had never seen before, nor shall ever again, for it is the most insipid, ridiculous play that I ever saw in my life.

Samuel Pepys, English diarist

Auden is an accomplished rhymer and Shakespeare is not.

Peter Porter, English poet

What's in a name, anyway? That which we call a nose by any other name would still smell.

Reduced Shakespeare Company, *The Compleat Works of Wllm Shkspr*

Oh, Blimey O'Riley's pantyhose ... What is the point of Shakespeare? I know he is a genius and so on, but he does rave on. 'What light doth through yonder window break?' It's the bloody moon, for God sake, Will, get a grip!

Louise Rennison, *Dancing in My Nuddy-Pants* (2002)

I have striven hard to open English eyes to the emptiness of Shakespeare's philosophy, to the superficiality and second-handedness of his morality, to his weakness and incoherence as a thinker, to his snobbery, his vulgar prejudices, his ignorance, his disqualifications of all sorts for the philosophic eminence claimed for him.

George Bernard Shaw, Irish playwright, 1906

With the single exception of Homer, there is no eminent writer, not even Sir Walter Scott, whom I can despise so entirely as I despise Shakespeare when I measure my mind against his. The intensity of my impatience with him occasionally reaches such a pitch, that it would positively be a relief to me to dig him up and throw stones at him, knowing as I do how incapable he and his worshippers are of understanding any less obvious form of indignity.

George Bernard Shaw, 1906

Crude, immoral, vulgar and senseless.

Leo Tolstoy, Russian novelist

This enormous dunghill...

Voltaire, French writer, historian and philosopher

I have been right, Basil, haven't I, to take my love out of poetry, and to find my wife in Shakespeare's plays? Lips that Shakespeare taught to speak have whispered their secret in my ear. I have had the arms of Rosalind around me, and kissed Juliet on the mouth.

Oscar Wilde, Irish writer, essayist and playwright

Actors are so fortunate. They can choose whether they will appear in tragedy or in comedy, whether they will suffer or make merry, laugh or shed tears. But in real life it is different. Most men and women are forced to perform parts for which they have no qualifications. Our Guildensterns play Hamlet for us, and our Hamlets have to jest like Prince Hal. The world is a stage, but the play is badly cast.

Oscar Wilde, *Lord Arthur Savile's Crime and Other Stories* (1891)

We've all heard that a million monkeys banging on a million typewriters will eventually reproduce the entire works of Shakespeare. Now, thanks to the Internet, we know this is not true.
    Robert Wilensky, computer science professor

As Shakespeare says, if you're going to do a thing you might as well pop right at it and get it over.
    P. G. Wodehouse, *Very Good, Jeeves!* (1930)

It was one of those cases where you approve the broad, general principle of an idea but can't help being in a bit of a twitter at the prospect of putting it into practical effect. I explained this to Jeeves, and he said much the same thing had bothered Hamlet.
    P. G. Wodehouse, *Jeeves in the Morning* (1946)

#SHAW, GEORGE BERNARD
1856–1950, Irish playwright

You ought to be roasted alive, though even then, you would not be to my taste.
    J. M. Barrie, Scottish author and dramatist, to George Bernard Shaw, Irish playwright

George Bernard Shaw uses the English language like a truncheon.
    Max Beerbohm, English writer and critic

Shaw's brain is a half-inch layer of champagne poured over a bucket of Methodist near-beer.

Benjamin de Cassères, American journalist, critic
and poet

The simplest clues to life escape him, as he scales impossible pinnacles of unnecessary thought, only to slip down the other side.

Edward Gordon Craig, English actor, director
and theorist

Mr Shaw is (I suspect) the only man on earth who has never written poetry.

G. K. Chesterton, English author

The first man to have cut a swathe through the theatre and left it strewn with virgins.

Frank Harris, English author and journalist

Shaw, most poisonous of all the poisonous haters of England, despiser, distorter and denier of the plain truths whereby men live; topsy-turvy perverter of all human relationships; a menace to ordered social thought and ordered social life; irresponsible braggart, blaring self-trumpeter.

Henry A. Jones, English dramatist

A good man fallen among Fabians.

Vladimir Ilyich Lenin, Russian communist revolu-
tionary and politician

It is his life work to announce the obvious in terms of the scandalous.

    H. L. Mencken, American humorist

He writes his plays for the ages – the ages between five and twelve.

    George Jean Nathan, American editor and drama critic

He writes like a Pakistani who had learned English when he was twelve years old in order to become a chartered accountant.

    John Osborne, English playwright, actor and critic

I remember coming across him at the Grand Canyon and finding him peevish, refusing to admire it or even look at it properly. He was jealous of it.

    J. B. Priestley, English novelist, playwright and
    broadcaster

Concerning no subject would Shaw be deterred by the minor accident of total ignorance from penning a definitive opinion.

    Roger Scruton, English critic and commentator

I never accepted a knighthood because to be me is honour enough.

    George Bernard Shaw

George Bernard Shaw, the spinster aunt of English literature.

    Kenneth Tynan, English critic

An idiot child screaming in a hospital.
   H. G. Wells, English novelist, historian and
   commentator

The more I think you over, the more it comes home to
me what an unmitigated Middle Victorian ass you are!
   H. G. Wells, to Shaw

An excellent man: he has no enemies, and none of his
friends like him.
   Oscar Wilde, Irish writer, essayist and playwright

The way Bernard Shaw believes in himself is very
refreshing in these atheistic days when so many people
believe in no God at all.
   Israel Zangwill, British humorist and writer

#SPEAKERS AND SPEECHES

His speeches left the impression of an army of pompous phrases moving over the landscape in search of
an idea.
   Anon.

The whole art of a political speech is to put *nothing*
into it. It is much more difficult than it sounds.
   Hilaire Belloc, *A Conversation with an Angel and
   Other Essays* (1928)

Drawing on my fine command of language, I said nothing.

    Robert Benchley, American humorist

CHAIRMAN: Chauncey Depew can always produce a speech. All you have to do is give him his dinner and up comes his speech.
CHAUNCEY DEPEW: I only hope that it isn't true that if I give you my speech, up will come your dinner.

    Chauncey Depew, nineteenth-century railroad execu-
    tive and US senator

Talk to people about themselves and they will listen for hours.

    Benjamin Disraeli, British Prime Minister 1868,
    1874–80

Everything becomes a little different as soon as it is spoken out loud.

    Hermann Hesse, German poet and painter

No man would listen to you talk if he didn't know it was his turn next.

    Edgar Watson Howe, American humorist

Hubert, a speech does not need to be eternal to be immortal.

    Muriel Humphrey, reminder to her husband Hubert
    H. Humphrey, former US Vice President

Most conversations are simply monologues delivered in the presence of a witness.

> Margaret Millar, American-Canadian writer

A good off-the-cuff informal speech takes more preparation than a formal speech.

> Richard M. Nixon, US President 1969–74, speech made in New York City, 1955

A political speech should be like a woman's skirt – long enough to be respectable and short enough to be interesting.

> Adam Clayton Powell, US Congressman

Sir Winston Churchill devoted the best years of his life to preparing his impromptu speeches.

> F. E. Smith, British Conservative politician

You spoke so flatteringly about me that for a moment I thought I was dead.

> Harry Truman, US President 1945–53, reacting to praise from Israeli ambassador Abba Eban

Today's public figures can no longer write their own speeches or books, and there is some evidence that they can't read them either.

> Gore Vidal, American critic and commentator

#SPELLING

Eye halve a spelling checker
It came with my Pea Sea,
It plane lee marks four my revue
Miss steaks aye dew knot sea.

Eye ran this poem threw it,
Your sure reel glad two no.
Its vary polished in it's weigh
My checker tolled me sew
  Anon., *An Owed Two The Spelling Checker*

It is a damn poor mind that can think of only one way
to spell a word.
  Andrew Jackson, US President 1829–37

If you can spell 'Nietzsche' without Google, you
deserve a cookie.
  Lauren Leto, American founder of website Texts from
  Last Night

#SPORT

Every sport pretends to a literature, but people don't
believe it of any other sport but their own.
  Alistair Cooke, British–American journalist and
  broadcaster

I once thought of becoming a political cartoonist because they only have to come up with one idea a day. Then I thought I'd become a sportswriter instead, because they don't have to come up with any.

Sam Snead, American golfer

#SUCCESS

It is wise to keep in mind that no success or failure is necessarily final.

Anon.

It is difficult to make a reputation, but it is even more difficult seriously to mar a reputation once properly made – so faithful is the public.

Arnold Bennett, English author and journalist

If you try to fail, and succeed, which have you done?

George Carlin, American comedian

Success consists of going from failure to failure without loss of enthusiasm.

Sir Winston Churchill, British Prime Minister
1940–45, 1951–5

There is no point at which you can say, 'Well, I'm successful now. I might as well take a nap.'

Carrie Fisher, American actress and novelist

For a writer, success is always temporary, success is only a delayed failure. And it is incomplete.
  Graham Greene, *A Sort of Life* (1971)

It is sobering to consider that when Mozart was my age he had already been dead for a year.
  Tom Lehrer, American satirical songwriter

The worst part of having success is to try finding someone who is happy for you.
  Bette Midler, American actress and singer

There's no point in success if you don't let it go to your head. That's what it's for.
  John Otway, British rock singer

The secret of success is to offend the greatest number of people.
  George Bernard Shaw, Irish playwright

It is fatal to be appreciated in one's own time.
  Osbert Sitwell, quoted in *The Observer*, 1924

All you need in this life is ignorance and confidence, and then success is sure.
  Mark Twain, letter, 1887

Failure is very difficult for a writer to bear, but very few can manage the shock of early success.
  Maurice Valency, American playwright, author
  and critic

Success comes to a writer, as a rule, so gradually that it is always something of a shock to him to look back and realise the heights to which he has climbed.

P. G. Wodehouse, English humorist

The usual drawback to success is that it annoys one's friends so.

P. G. Wodehouse, *The Man Upstairs* (1914)

T

#TRANSLATION

Angry Raisins.
   Japanese bookshop's translation of *The Grapes of Wrath* by John Steinbeck

#TWAIN, MARK
1835–1910, American author and humorist

The rule is perfect: in all matters of opinion our adversaries are insane.
   Mark Twain

Persons attempting to find a motive in this narrative will be prosecuted, persons attempting to find a moral in it will be punished; persons attempting to find a plot in it will be shot.
   Mark Twain, *The Adventures of Huckleberry Finn* (1884)

My books are water; those of the great geniuses is wine. Everybody drinks water.

Mark Twain, *Notebook* (1935), ed. by Albert Bigelow Paine

#TWITTER

Twitter: proudly promoting ghastly grammar and silly misspelling since 2006.

E. A. Bucchianeri, American author

When you've got 5 minutes to fill, Twitter is a great way to fill 35 minutes.

Matt Cutts, 2013

Q: What happened after hackers shut down Twitter for a day?
A: Twitterers were relegated to communicating the old fashioned way. Through Facebook!

www.jokes4us.com

The Republican presidential candidates held a debate on Twitter. It combined the excitement of C-SPAN with the suspense of typing.

Jimmy Kimmel Live, ABC

David Letterman's Top Ten Signs You Spend Too Much Time on Twitter
10. You miss son's soccer game waiting for Lady Gaga to post what she had for lunch

9. You answer the phone: 'Twello?'
8. You've spent millions developing iPhone water-proofing technology so you can tweet in the shower
7. You haven't touched your CB radio in months
6. You ask yourself, 'What would Jesus tweet?'
5. You sleep-tweet
4. No No. 4 – writer on Twitter
3. You stopped paying attention to this list after the first 140 characters
2. Even Ashton Kutcher thinks you tweet too much
1. Walked in on the landscaper 'retweeting' your wife.
    David Letterman, *The Late Show*, CBS

A man tells his doctor, 'Doc, help me. I'm addicted to Twitter!'
    The doctor replies, 'Sorry, I don't follow you...'
    Reader's Digest, 2013

W

#WAUGH, EVELYN
1903–66, English novelist

If *Brideshead Revisited* is not a great book, it's so like
a great book that many of us, at least while reading it,
find it hard to tell the difference.
  Clive James, Australian critic

The lady said, 'It's no good trying to buy a paper here.
That Sir William Beveridge is going to abolish want,
so all the papers were sold out.' Later that day or the
next day I asked him to come to lunch. I was meet-
ing with Evelyn Waugh, an old friend and famous
writer. They did not get on at all well. Evelyn Waugh
said to him at the end, 'How do you get your main
pleasure in life, Sir William?' He paused and said, 'I
get mine trying to leave the world a better place than
I found it.' Evelyn Waugh said, 'I get mine spreading
alarm and despondency' – this was in the height of the
war – 'and I get more satisfaction than you do.' So he
did not meet with universal acclamation, but nearly

everyone admired Beveridge at that time. He was a
wonderful man.

Lord Longford, English aristocrat, politician and
social reformer

#WILDE, OSCAR
1854–1900, Irish writer, essayist and playwright

From the beginning Wilde performed his life and
continued to do so even after fate had taken the plot
out of his hands.

W. H. Auden, Anglo-American poet, *The New Yorker*,
1963

An Assyrian wax statue, effeminate, but with the vital-
ity of twenty men.

Max Beerbohm, English writer and critic

That sovereign of insufferables, Oscar Wilde has
ensued with his opulence of twaddle and his penury
of sense. He has mounted his hind legs and blown
crass vapidities through the bowel of his neck, to the
capital edification of circumjacent fools and foolesses,
fooling with their foolers. He has tossed off the top
of his head and uttered himself in copious overflows of
ghastly bosh. The ineffable dunce has nothing to say
and says it – says it with a liberal embellishment of
bad delivery, embroidering it with reasonless vulgari-
ties of attitude, gesture and attire. There never was an
impostor so hateful, a blockhead so stupid, a crank

so variously and offensively daft. Therefore is the she-fool enamored of the feel of his tongue in her ear to tickle her understanding.

The limpid and spiritless vacuity of this intellectual jellyfish is in ludicrous contrast with the rude but robust mental activities that he came to quicken and inspire. Not only has he no thoughts, but no thinker. His lecture is mere verbal ditch-water – meaningless, trite and without coherence. It lacks even the nasti-ness that exalts and refines his verse. Moreover, it is obviously his own; he had not even the energy and independence to steal it. And so, with a knowledge that would equip an idiot to dispute with a cast-iron dog, and eloquence to qualify him for the duties of a caller on a hog-ranch, and an imagination adequate to the conception of a tom-cat, when fired by contempla-tion of a fiddle-string, this consummate and star-like youth, missing everywhere his heaven-appointed func-tions and offices, wanders about, posing as a statue of himself, and, like the sun-smitten image of Memnon, emitting meaningless murmurs in the blaze of women's eyes.

He makes me tired. And this gawky gowk has the divine effrontery to link his name with those of Swinburne, Rossetti and Morris – this dunghill he-hen would fly with eagles. He dares to set his tongue to the honored name of Keats. He is the leader, quoth'a, of a renaissance in art, this man who cannot draw – of a revival of letters, this man who cannot write! This little and looniest of a brotherhood of simpletons, whom the wicked wits of London, haling him dazed from his obscurity, have crowned and crucified as King of the Cranks, has accepted the distinction in stupid good faith and our foolish people take him at his word. Mr Wilde is pinnacled upon a dazzling eminence but the earth still trembles to the dull thunder of the kicks that set him up.

Ambrose Bierce, *Wasp* magazine, San Francisco, 1882

No man, so capable of thinking about truth and beauty, ever thought so constantly about his own effect on the middle classes ... One might go through his swift and sparkling plays with a red and blue pencil marking two kinds of epigrams; the real epigram which he wrote to please his own wild intellect, and the sham epigram which he wrote to thrill the very tamest part of our tame civilisation.

G. K. Chesterton, *Daily News*, 1909

What a tiresome, affected sod.

Noël Coward, English playwright and entertainer

He festooned the dung heap on which he had placed himself with sonnets as people who grow honeysuckle around outdoor privies.

Quentin Crisp, English writer

Oscar Wilde was over-dressed, pompous, snobbish, sentimental and vain.

Evelyn Waugh, English novelist

I put all my genius into my life; I put only my talent into my works.
    Oscar Wilde

I am so clever that sometimes I don't understand a single word of what I am saying.
    Oscar Wilde

I have the simplest tastes. I am always satisfied with the best.
    Oscar Wilde

#WOMEN AND WRITING

A woman, especially if she have the misfortune of knowing anything, should conceal it as well as she can.
    Jane Austen, English novelist

No man should ever publish a book until he has first read it to a woman.
    Van Wyck Brooks, American critic and biographer

Men are from Earth, women are from Earth. Deal with it.
    George Carlin, American comedian

Most books on witchcraft will tell you that witches work naked. This is because most books on witchcraft were written by men.
    Neil Gaiman, English science fiction author

All women as authors are feeble and tiresome. I wish they were forbidden to write, on pain of having their faces deeply scarified with an oyster shell.
> Nathaniel Hawthorne, American novelist and short story writer, letter to his publisher

Beware of the man who denounces women writers – his penis is tiny and he can't spell.
> Erica Jong, American writer and teacher

A study in the *Washington Post* says that women have better verbal skills than men. I just want to say to the authors of that study: 'Duh.'
> Conan O'Brien, American comedian

One of the surest signs of his genius is that women dislike his books.
> George Orwell, English writer and commentator, on Joseph Conrad, Polish author

The solitary genius in the garret is a male myth, as he would undoubtedly have been supported by several unacknowledged women who cooked and ironed.
> Michèle Roberts, British novelist and poet, 1996

Literature cannot be the business of a woman's life, because of the sacredness of her duties at home.
> Robert Southey, English Romantic poet, on Charlotte Brontë, English novelist

There are men who fear repartee in a wife more keenly than a sword.

P. G. Wodehouse, *Jill the Reckless* (1921)

#WORDS

If there's one word that sums up everything that's gone wrong since the war, it's 'workshop'.

Kingsley Amis, *Jake's Thing* (1978)

Remember, the plural of 'moron' is 'focus group'.

Anon.

The word 'duck' is 75 per cent obscene.

Lenny Bruce, American comedian, social critic and satirist

The word 'good' has many meanings. For example, if a man were to shoot his grandmother at a range of 500 yards, I should call him a good shot, but not necessarily a good man.

G. K. Chesterton, English author

Why shouldn't we quarrel about a word? What is the good of words if they aren't important enough to quarrel over? Why do we choose one word more than another if there isn't any difference between them?

G. K. Chesterton

Broadly speaking, the short words are the best, and the old words best of all.
  Sir Winston Churchill, British Prime Minister
  1940–45, 1951–5

I wonder whether any woman could be happy with a man who says 'folderol'.
  Peter De Vries, American novelist

When I was at school I learned to spell the word 'myrrh'. I have never had cause to write the word again.
  Tony Hawks, English comedian

'Fragile' is usually interpreted by postal workers as 'please throw underarm'.
  Harry Hershfield, American cartoonist, comedian and
  radio personality

I would never use a long word where a short one would answer the purpose. I know there are professors in this country who 'ligate' arteries. Other surgeons only tie them, and it stops the bleeding just as well.
  Oliver Wendell Holmes, American poet and physician

The word 'meaningful' when used today is nearly always meaningless.
  Paul Johnson, *The Observer*, 1982

It should be a law that if you use the word 'paradigm' without knowing what it means, you go to jail. No exceptions.
  Dave Jones, American comedian (attrib.)

If the English language made any sense, lackadaisical would have something to do with a shortage of flowers.
  Doug Larson, American editor and columnist

Some people have a way with words, and other people … oh, uh, not have way.
  Steve Martin, American actor and comedian

Et cetera – the expression that makes people think you know more than you do.
  Herbert Prochnow, American banker

I don't think writers are sacred, but words are. They deserve respect. If you get the right ones in the right order, you can nudge the world a little or make a poem which children will speak for you when you're dead.
  Tom Stoppard, *The Real Thing: A Play* (1982)

Whom is a word invented to make everyone sound like a butler.
  Calvin Trillin, American journalist and poet

#WRITERS

After being turned down by numerous publishers, he decided to write for posterity.
  George Ade, *Fables in Slang* (1899)

I began as a writer as soon as I left university and within six months I'd sold several articles – my watch, my overcoat, my typewriter...
    Anon.

T. S. Eliot is quite at a loss
When clubwomen bustle across
At literary teas
Crying: – 'What, if you please,
Did you mean by The Mill on the Floss'
    W. H. Auden, 'T. S. Eliot', *Collected Poems* (1977)

We're all miners in our family. My father was a miner. My mother *is* a miner. These are miner's hands. We're all artists I suppose, really, only I was the first one who had this urge to express myself on paper rather than at the coal face. But under the skin I think I'm still a miner. I suppose in a very real sense I'm a miner writer.
    Alan Bennett, 'The Lonely Pursuit', *On the Margin*,
    BBC TV, 1966

Of all the honours that fell upon Virginia's [Woolf] head, none, I think, pleased her more than the *Evening Standard* Award for the Tallest Woman Writer of 1927, an award she took by a neck from Elizabeth Bowen. And rightly, I think, for she was in a very real sense the tallest writer I have known. Which is not to say that her stories were tall. They were not. They were short. But she did stand head and shoulders above her contemporaries, and sometimes of course, much more so.
    Alan Bennett, *Forty Years On* (1968)

In America only the successful writer is important, in France all writers are important, in England no writer is important, in Australia you have to explain what a writer is.

Geoffrey Cotterell, English novelist and wit

Some day I hope to write a book where the royalties will pay for the copies I give away.

Clarence Darrow, American lawyer

My aged friend, Mrs Wilkinson,
Whose mother was a Lambe,
Saw Wordsworth once, and Coleridge, too,
One morning in her p'ram
Birdlike the bards stooped over her –
Like fledgling in a nest:
And Wordsworth said, 'Thou harmless babe!'
And Coleridge was impressed.
The pretty thing gazed up and smiled,
And softly murmured, 'Coo!'
William was then aged sixty-four
And Samuel sixty-two.

Walter de la Mare, 'The Bards'

Most writers are vain, so I try to ensure that any author who comes to stay will find at least one of their books in their room.

The Duke of Devonshire

They're fancy talkers about themselves, writers. If I had to give young writers advice, I would say don't listen to writers talk about writing or themselves.

    Lillian Hellman, American author and memoirist

To want to meet an author because you like his books is as ridiculous as wanting to meet the goose because you like pâté de foie gras.

    Arthur Koestler, Hungarian–British author and
    journalist

I've just seen P. Herbert!
Not THE P. Herbert?
No, just A. P. Herbert!

    Fred Metcalf, English encyclopedist

Almost anyone can be an author; the business is to collect money and fame from this state of being.

    A. A. Milne, English writer

Oscar and George Bernard
Cannot be reconciled.
When I'm Wilde about Shaw
I'm not Shaw about Wilde.

    Frederick Oliver, *Worse Verse* (1969)

When one says that a writer is fashionable one practically always means that he is admired by people under thirty.

    George Orwell, English writer and commentator

My brother's a failed author. He writes books nobody wants to read and cheques nobody wants to cash.

Sally Poplin, English writer

He's been a writer ever since he was a teenager. In fact, as soon as he left school he began to write for money – in every letter his parents got from him.

Sally Poplin

He's a writer whose books will be read long after Shakespeare, Dickens and Henry James are forgotten. But not until then.

Sally Poplin

It is part of prudence to thank an author for his book before reading it, so as to avoid the necessity of lying about it afterwards.

George Santayana, Spanish-born philosopher, author and poet

The profession of book writing makes horse racing seem like a solid, stable business.

John Steinbeck, American novelist

Some American writers who have known each other for years have never met in the daytime or when both were sober.

James Thurber, American comic writer

One editor said to me, 'You could be the next Dorothy Parker.'

I thought, 'What? Keep slashing my wrists and drinking shoe polish?'

Lynne Truss, author of *Eats, Shoots & Leaves: The Zero Tolerance Approach to Punctuation* (2003)

See also #WRITER'S LIFE, THE, #WRITERS ON THEMSELVES, #WRITERS ON WRITERS

#WRITER'S BLOCK

I am not at all in a humour for writing; I must write on till I am.

Jane Austen, English novelist

'I have writer's block. It's the worst feeling in the world.'

'Try ten days without a bowel movement sometime.'

The Golden Girls, NBC

Writer's block is a disease for which there is no cure, only respite.

Terri Guillemets, collector of quotes

Writer's block is only a failure of the ego.

Norman Mailer, American writer and film-maker

Writer's block is a fancy term made up by whiners so they can have an excuse to drink alcohol.

Steve Martin, American actor and comedian

Writer's block ... a lot of howling nonsense would be avoided if, in every sentence containing the word WRITER, that word was taken out and the word PLUMBER substituted; and the result examined for the sense it makes. Do plumbers get plumber's block? What would you think of a plumber who used that as an excuse not to do any work that day?

The fact is that writing is hard work, and sometimes you don't want to do it, and you can't think of what to write next, and you're fed up with the whole damn business. Do you think plumbers don't feel like that about their work from time to time? Of course there will be days when the stuff is not flowing freely. What you do then is MAKE IT UP. I like the reply of the composer Shostakovich to a student who complained that he couldn't find a theme for his second movement. 'Never mind the theme! Just write the movement!' he said.

Writer's block is a condition that affects amateurs and people who aren't serious about writing. So is the opposite, namely inspiration, which amateurs are also very fond of. Putting it another way: a professional writer is someone who writes just as well when they're not inspired as when they are.

Philip Pullman, English author

Nothing's a better cure for writer's block than to eat ice cream right out of the carton.

Don Roff, American writer and film-maker

#WRITER'S LIFE, THE

I read about writers' lives with the fascination of one slowing down to get a good look at an automobile accident.
   Kaye Gibbons, American novelist

You know, it's not exactly a natural pursuit, a man putting himself in front of a typewriter – a machine – day after day. But you've got to spend three or four years digging yourself a rut so deep that finally you find it more convenient not to get out of it.
   Ernest Haycox, American author of Western fiction

No author dislikes to be edited as much as he dislikes not to be published.
   Russell Lynes, American art historian and author

It's not a good idea to put your wife into a novel – not your latest wife, anyway.
   Norman Mailer, American writer and film-maker

This writing business. Pencils and whatnot. Overrated if you ask me.
   A. A. Milne, *Winnie-the-Pooh* (attrib.)

He is a man of thirty-five, but looks fifty. He is bald, has varicose veins and wears spectacles, or would wear them if his only pair were not chronically lost. If things are normal with him, he will be suffering from malnutrition, but if he has recently had a lucky streak, he will be suffering from a hangover. At present it is half past eleven in the morning, and according to his schedule he should have started work two hours ago; but even if he had made any serious effort to start he would have been frustrated by the almost continuous ringing of the telephone bell, the yells of the baby, the rattle of an electric drill out in the street, and the heavy boots of his creditors clumping up the stairs. The most recent interruption was the arrival of the second post, which brought him two circulars and an income tax demand printed in red. Needless to say this person is a writer.

George Orwell, 'Confessions of a Book Reviewer' (1946)

Writing is not a profession but a vocation of unhappiness.

Georges Simenon, Belgian author

Eighty per cent work and worry over work, struggle against lunacy ten per cent and friends one per cent.

Tennessee Williams, American playwright, giving a breakdown of his life

#WRITERS ON THEMSELVES

My face looks like a wedding cake that has been left out in the rain.

W. H. Auden, Anglo-American poet

The only thing I was fit for was to be a writer, and this notion rested solely on my suspicion that I would never be fit for real work, and that writing didn't require any.

Russell Baker, American writer and satirist

I called my first book *The Collected Works of Max Beerbohm, Volume One.*

Max Beerbohm, English writer and critic

I am a drinker with a writing problem.

Brendan Behan, Irish novelist and playwright

I am writing a book about the Crusades so dull that I can scarcely write it.

Hilaire Belloc, English writer

There was a time when I thought my only connection to the literary world would be that I once delivered meat to T. S. Eliot's mother in law.

Alan Bennett, English diarist and playwright

The ideal reader of my novels is a lapsed Catholic and a failed musician, short-sighted, colour-blind, auditorily biased who has read the books that I have read. He should also be about my age.

Anthony Burgess, English novelist, 1977

The book I would most like to have with me on a desert island is *Thomas's Guide to Practical Shipbuilding*.
    G. K. Chesterton, English author

I am as shallow as a puddle.
    Helen Fielding, author of *Bridget Jones's Diary*

I am irritated by my own writing. I am like a violinist whose ear is true, but whose fingers refuse to reproduce precisely the sound he hears within.
    Gustave Flaubert, French novelist

Unprovided with original learning, unformed in the habits of thinking, unskilled in the arts of composition, I resolved to write a book.
    Edward Gibbon, English historian

I can write better than anyone who can write faster, and I can write faster than anyone who can write better.
    A. J. Liebling, *New Yorker* journalist

My Opus Number one cost me an unconscionable quantity of paper and was called, with merciless fitness, *Immaturity*. Part of it was devoured by mice, though even they had not been able to finish it.
    George Bernard Shaw, Irish playwright

I'm a jobbing writer, like everyone else.
    Fay Weldon, English novelist, explaining why she did work for a jewellery company

It scarcely needs criticism to bring home to me that much of my work has been slovenly, haggard and irritated, most of it hurriedly and inadequately revised, and some of it as white and pasty as a starch-fed nun.
  H. G. Wells, *Experiment in Autobiography* (1934)

See also #WRITERS, #WRITER'S LIFE, THE, #WRITERS ON WRITERS

#WRITERS ON WRITERS

No poet or novelist wishes he were the only one who ever lived, but most of them wish they were the only one alive, and quite a number fondly believe their wish has been granted.
  W. H. Auden, Anglo-American poet

A professional writer is an amateur who didn't quit.
  Richard Bach, American author

It's all very well to be able to write books, but can you waggle your ears?
  J. M. Barrie, Scottish author, to H. G. Wells, English novelist, historian and commentator

You shouldn't pay any attention to anything writers say. They don't know why they do what they do. They're like good tennis players or good painters, who are just full of nonsense, pompous and embarrassing.
  John Barth, American novelist and short story writer, 1972

Byron! He would be all forgotten today if he had lived to be a florid old gentleman with iron-grey whiskers, writing very long, very able letters to *The Times* about the repeal of the Corn Laws.

> Max Beerbohm, English writer and critic, on the
> English Romantic poet

I thought that there could be only two worse writers than Stephen Crane, namely two Stephen Cranes.

> Ambrose Bierce, on fellow American author

H. L. Mencken suffers from the delusion that he is H. L. Mencken. There is no cure for a disease of that magnitude.

> Maxwell Bodenheim, American poet and novelist, on
> the American humorist

Edward Gibbon is an ugly, affected, disgusting fellow and poisons our literary club for me. I class him among infidel wasps and venomous insects.

> James Boswell, Scottish lawyer and diarist, on the
> English historian

The stupid person's idea of a clever person.

> Elizabeth Bowen, Irish novelist and short story writer,
> on English writer Aldous Huxley

Henry Miller is not really a writer but a non-stop talker to whom someone has given a typewriter.

> Gerald Brenan, British writer and Hispanist, on the
> American writer

Balzac was so conceited that he raised his hat every time he spoke of himself.
    Robert Broughton, on the French novelist

To those she did not like, she was a stiletto made of sugar.
    John Mason Brown, American critic and author, on
    Dorothy Parker, American wit

Writers are desperate people and when they stop being desperate they stop being writers.
    Charles Bukowski, American poet

It was very good of God to let Carlyle and Mrs Carlyle marry one another and so make only two people miserable instead of four.
    Samuel Butler, English author and satirist, on Scottish
    historian Thomas Carlyle and his wife

Who invited him in? What was he doing here,
That insolent little ruffian, that crapulous lout?
When he quitted a sofa, he left behind him a smear.
My wife says he even tried to paw her about.
    Norman Cameron, Scottish poet, on Welsh poet
    Dylan Thomas

You can't blame a writer for what the characters say.
    Truman Capote, American writer and journalist

I knew William Faulkner well. He was a great friend of mine. Well, as much as you could be a friend of his, unless you were a fourteen-year-old nymphet.
    Truman Capote, on fellow American author

That's not writing – that's typing.
  Truman Capote, on fellow American author Jack
  Kerouac

Self-knowledge does not necessarily help a novelist.
It helps a human being a great deal but novelists are
often appalling human beings.
  Peter Carey, Australian novelist

Most writers have the egotism of actors with none of
the good looks or charm.
  Raymond Chandler, American novelist and screenwriter, 1948

Times are bad. Children no longer obey their parents,
and everyone is writing a book.
  Marcus Tullius Cicero, Roman philosopher and
  politician, 43 BC

Writers are always selling somebody out.
  Joan Didion, American novelist

Writers should be read, but neither seen nor heard.
  Daphne du Maurier, English author and playwright

Writers should be read and not seen. Rarely are they a
winsome sight.
  Edna Ferber, American novelist and playwright

It is splendid to be a great writer, to put men into the frying pan of your words and make them pop like chestnuts.

Gustave Flaubert, French novelist, 1851

Most people who seek attention and regards by announcing that they're writing a novel are actually so devoid of narrative talent that they can't hold the attention of a dinner table for thirty seconds, even with a dirty joke.

Paul Fussell, American historian and author

That's Kingsley Amis and there's no known cure.

Robert Graves, English poet, on the English novelist, poet and critic

As a child I was an inveterate liar. As opposed to now, I am a Novelist.

John Green, American writer and educator

Every writer I know has trouble writing.

Joseph Heller, American novelist, short story writer and playwright

A little talent is a good thing to have if you want to be a writer. But the only real requirement is the ability to remember every scar.

Stephen King, American novelist

A writer is someone for whom writing is more difficult than it is for other people.

Thomas Mann, *Essays of Three Decades* (1947)

I think if a third of all novelists and maybe two thirds of all the poets now writing dropped dead suddenly, their loss to literature would not be great.

Charles Osborne (attrib.)

I am a strong believer in the tyranny, the dictatorship, the absolute authority of the writer.

Philip Pullman, English author

Writers, those professionals of dissatisfaction.

Susan Sontag, American writer and activist, 2001

Teaching has ruined more American novelists than drink.

Gore Vidal, American critic and commentator

What a nightmare, to wake up in the morning and realise that you are John Simon.

Gore Vidal, on a renowned literary critic

With a pig's eyes that never look up, with a pig's snout that loves muck, with a pig's brain that knows only the sty, and with a pig's squeal that cries only when he is hurt, he sometimes opens his pig's mouth, tusked and ugly, and lets out the voice of God, railing at the whitewash that covers the manure about his habitat.

William Allen White, American editor, writer and politician, on H. L. Mencken, American humorist, 1928

I hate vulgar realism in literature. The man who would call a spade a spade should be compelled to use one. It is the only thing he is fit for.
   Oscar Wilde, *The Picture of Dorian Gray* (1891)

A writer's mind seems to be situated partly in the solar plexus and partly in the head.
   Ethel Wilson, Canadian novelist

… the dullest speeches I ever heard. The Agee woman told us for three quarters of an hour how she came to write her beastly book, when a simple apology was all that was required.
   P. G. Wodehouse, *The Girl in Blue* (1970)

See #WRITERS ON THEMSELVES, #WRITERS VERSUS CRITICS

#WRITERS ON WRITING

I love deadlines. I love the whooshing noise they make as they go by.
   Douglas Adams, *The Salmon of Doubt* (2002)

The art of writing is the art of applying the seat of one's pants to the seat of one's chair.
   Kingsley Amis, English novelist

If my doctor told me I had only six minutes to live, I wouldn't brood. I'd type a little faster.
   Isaac Asimov, American writer

Everyone thinks that writers must know more about the inside of the human head, but that is wrong. They know less, that's why they write: trying to find out what other people take for granted.
Margaret Atwood, *Dancing Girls and Other Stories* (1977)

Publishing a book is often very much like being put on trial for some offence which is quite other than the one you know in your heart you've committed.
Margaret Atwood, *Negotiating with the Dead* (2002)

How one likes to suffer. Anyway writers do; it is their income.
W. H. Auden, Anglo-American poet, 1929

Listen to the editor and nod – then put it back later.
Whitney Balliett, *New Yorker* critic and book reviewer

I am a galley slave to pen and ink.
Honoré de Balzac, French novelist

All a writer has to do to get a woman is to say he's a writer. It's an aphrodisiac.
Saul Bellow, American novelist

You never have to change anything you got up in the middle of the night to write.
Saul Bellow

You have to know how to accept rejection and reject acceptance.

Ray Bradbury, American novelist, essayist and poet

Just write every day of your life. Read intensely. Then see what happens. Most of my friends who are put on that diet have very pleasant careers.

Ray Bradbury

I don't believe in being serious about anything. I think life is too serious to be taken seriously.

Ray Bradbury

I'm working when I'm fighting with my wife. I constantly ask myself, 'How can I use this stuff to literary advantage?'

Art Buchwald, American columnist

Don't ever write a novel unless it hurts like a hot turd coming out.

Charles Bukowski, American poet and novelist

When you write down your life, every page should contain something no one has ever heard about.

Elias Canetti, Bulgarian novelist and playwright

I believe more in the scissors than I do in the pencil.

Truman Capote, American writer and journalist

Metaphors have a way of holding the most truth in the least space.

Orson Scott Card, American author, essayist and activist

Most of the basic material a writer works with is acquired before the age of fifteen.

Willa Cather, American novelist

You could compile the worst book in the world entirely out of selected passages from the best writers in the world.

G. K. Chesterton, English author

I've always believed in writing without a collaborator because, where two people are writing the same book, each believes he gets all the worries and only half the royalties.

Agatha Christie, British crime writer

The best time for planning a book is while you're doing the dishes.

Agatha Christie

Writing a book is an adventure. To begin with, it is a toy and an amusement; then it becomes a mistress, and then it becomes a master, and then a tyrant. The last phase is that just as you are about to be reconciled to your servitude, you kill the monster, and fling him out to the public.

Sir Winston Churchill, British Prime Minister 1940–45, 1951–5

Novels should exclude all women with a nape to their necks.
Cyril Connolly, English critic and writer

I love being a writer. What I can't stand is the paperwork.
Peter De Vries, American novelist

I write when I'm inspired, and I see to it that I'm inspired at nine o'clock every morning.
Peter De Vries

Writing is like driving at night in the fog. You can only see as far as your headlights, but you can make the whole trip that way.
E. L. Doctorow, American author, 1988

Some editors are failed writers, but so are most writers.
T. S. Eliot, American poet and critic

Finish each day before you begin the next, and interpose a solid wall of sleep between the two. This you cannot do without temperance.
Ralph Waldo Emerson, American essayist and poet

The tools I need for my trade are paper, tobacco, food and a little whiskey.
William Faulkner, American novelist

The ideal view for daily writing, hour on hour, is the blank brick wall of a cold storage warehouse. Failing this, a stretch of sky will do, cloudless if possible.

Edna Ferber, American novelist and playwright

A writer wastes nothing.

F. Scott Fitzgerald, American novelist

Mostly, we authors must repeat ourselves – that's the truth. We have two or three great moving experiences in our lives – experiences so great and moving that it doesn't seem at the time that anyone else has been caught up and pounded and dazzled and astonished and beaten and broken and rescued and illuminated and rewarded and humbled in just that way ever before.

F. Scott Fitzgerald

Begin with an individual and you find that you have created a type; begin with a type and you find that you have created – nothing.

F. Scott Fitzgerald

All good writing is swimming under water and holding your breath.

F. Scott Fitzgerald

Once our work is printed – farewell! It belongs to everyone. It is the height of prostitution, and the vilest kind.

Gustave Flaubert, French novelist

Only the habit of persistent work can make one continually content; it produces an opium that numbs the soul.
  Gustave Flaubert, letter, 1851

The thing all writers do best is find ways to avoid writing.
  Alan Dean Foster, American science fiction writer

Writing is easy; all you do is sit staring at a blank sheet of paper until the drops of blood form on your forehead.
  Gene Fowler, American journalist and dramatist

This is how you do it: you sit down at the keyboard and you put one word after another until it's done. It's that easy, and that hard.
  Neil Gaiman, English science fiction author

7.44 am beginning the fourth draft, also known as the sick of the sight of every word draft.
  Linda Grant, English novelist, tweet, 2013

There is a splinter of ice in the heart of a writer.
  Graham Greene, English novelist

I've had secrets come out of my typewriter in invisible ink.
  Terri Guillemets, collector of quotes

Ink and paper are sometimes passionate lovers, oftentimes brother and sister, and occasionally mortal enemies.

Terri Guillemets

Loafing is the most productive part of a writer's life.

James Norman Hall, American author

Easy reading is damn hard writing.

Nathaniel Hawthorne, American novelist and short story writer

Writing is not necessarily something to be ashamed of, but do it in private and wash your hands afterwards.

Robert A. Heinlein, American science fiction writer

If I had to give young writers advice, I would say don't listen to writers talking about writing.

Lillian Hellman, American author and memoirist

Nothing you write, if you hope to be good, will ever come out as you first hoped.

Lillian Hellman

We are all apprentices in a craft where no one ever becomes a master.

Ernest Hemingway, American novelist and journalist

It's none of their business that you have to learn to write. Let them think you were born that way.
    Ernest Hemingway

The most essential gift for a good writer is a built-in shock-proof shit-detector.
    Ernest Hemingway

Unfortunately for novelists, real life is getting way too funny and far-fetched. It's especially true in Miami where the daily news seems to be scripted by David Lynch. Fact is routinely more fantastic than fiction.
    Carl Hiaasen, American novelist and journalist

The hardest thing is writing a recommendation for someone you know.
    Kin Hubbard, American wit

The most valuable of all talents is that of never using two words when one will do.
    Thomas Jefferson, US President 1801–9

Read over your compositions, and where ever you meet with a passage which you think is particularly fine, strike it out.
    Samuel Johnson, English poet, biographer and
    lexicographer

No man but a blockhead ever wrote, except for money.
    Samuel Johnson

Writing is like the world's oldest profession. First you do it for your own enjoyment. Then you do it for a few friends. Eventually, you figure, what the hell, I might as well get paid for it.

 Irma Kalish, American comedy writer

I write for *Reader's Digest*. It's not hard. All you do is copy out an article and mail it in again.

 Milt Kamen, American comedian

It ain't whatcha write, it's the way atcha write it.

 Jack Kerouac, American author

Write. Rewrite. When not writing or rewriting, read. I know of no shortcuts.

 Larry L. King, American journalist, novelist and
 playwright

So far as good writing goes, the use of the exclamation mark is a sign of failure. It is the literary equivalent of a man holding up a card reading LAUGHTER to a studio audience.

 Miles Kington, British journalist, musician and
 broadcaster, *Punch*, 1976

How do I like to write? With a soft pencil and a hard dick.

 Hanif Kureishi, English playwright and novelist

A good many young writers make the mistake of enclosing a stamped, self-addressed envelope, big enough for the manuscript to come back in. This is too much of a temptation for the editor.

Ring Lardner, *How to Write Short Stories* (1924)

I like to write when I feel spiteful; it's like having a good sneeze.

D. H. Lawrence, English novelist, poet and playwright, letter, 1913

If it sounds like writing, I rewrite it.

Elmore Leonard, American crime writer

The most important advice I would suggest to beginning writers: Try to leave out the parts that readers skip.

Elmore Leonard

The secret of writing great literature is to be under house arrest.

George Lukács, Hungarian Marxist philosopher

I get up in the morning with an idea for a three-volume novel and by nightfall it's a paragraph in my column.

Don Marquis, American humorist

If you want to get rich from writing, write the sort of thing that's read by persons who move their lips when they're reading to themselves.

Don Marquis

There are three rules for writing the novel. Unfortunately, no one knows what they are.
  W. Somerset Maugham, English playwright, novelist
  and short story writer

A good style should show no signs of effort. What is written should seem a happy accident.
  W. Somerset Maugham, *Summing Up* (1938)

I'm not a very good writer, but I'm an excellent rewriter.
  James Michener, American novelist

I get up in the morning and write. Then I tear it up. That's the routine.
  Arthur Miller, American playwright and essayist

I became a writer in the same way that a woman becomes a prostitute. First I did it to please myself, then I did it to please my friends, and finally I did it for money.
  Ferenc Molnar, Hungarian-born dramatist and
  and novelist

Being a writer blows. It's like having homework every day for the rest of your life.
  Hank Moody, *Californication*, Showtime

Writing is like getting married. One should never commit oneself until one is amazed at one's luck.
  Iris Murdoch, English novelist

Only ambitious nonentities and hearty mediocrities exhibit their rough drafts. It's like passing around samples of one's own sputum.

Vladimir Nabokov, Russian novelist

My writing is like fine wine; the more you read, the more you get from it. Reading it once is like taking a dog to the theatre.

V. S. Naipaul, Trinidadian–British novelist

Writing became such a process of discovery that I couldn't wait to get to work in the morning: I wanted to know what I was going to say.

Sharon O'Brien, American author

Everywhere I go I'm asked if I think the university stifles writers. My opinion is that they don't stifle enough of them. There's many a bestseller that could have been prevented by a good teacher.

Flannery O'Connor, American writer

I write because I don't know what I think until I read what I say.

Flannery O'Connor

Writing a novel is a terrible experience, during which the hair often falls out and the teeth decay. I'm always irritated by people who imply that writing fiction is an escape from reality. It is a plunge into reality and it's very shocking to the system.

Flannery O'Connor

From the time I was nine or ten, it was a toss-up whether I was going to be a writer or a painter, and I discovered by the time I was sixteen or seventeen that paints costs too much money, so I became a writer because you could be a writer with a pencil and a penny notebook.

Frank O'Connor, Irish novelist and short story writer, 1989

The point of heterosexual male literature, art, music, science and rugby is to win the love of women.

Redmond O'Hanlon, English writer and scholar

Writing a book is a horrible, exhausting struggle, like a long bout of some painful illness. One would never undertake such a thing if one were not driven on by some demon whom one can neither resist nor understand.

George Orwell, English writer and commentator

I hate writing, I love having written.

Dorothy Parker, American wit

The writer's way is rough and lonely, and who would choose it while there are vacancies in more gracious professions such as, say, cleaning out ferryboats?

Dorothy Parker

I have made this letter longer than usual, only because I have not had the time to make it shorter.

Blaise Pascal, French writer and philosopher

A word is not the same with one writer as with another. One tears it from his guts. The other pulls it out of his overcoat pocket.

    Charles Péguy, French poet, essayist and editor

After nourishment, shelter and companionship, stories are the thing we need most in the world.

    Philip Pullman, English author

What no wife of a writer can ever understand is that a writer is working when he's staring out of the window.

    Burton Rascoe, American journalist and editor

If you caricature friends in your first novel they will be upset, but if you don't, they will feel betrayed.

    Mordecai Richler, *GQ*, 1984

You can fix anything but a blank page.

    Nora Roberts, American romance novelist

I asked Ring Lardner the other day how he writes his short stories, and he said he wrote a few widely separated words or phrases on a piece of paper and then went back and filled in the spaces.

    Harold Ross, *New Yorker* journalist

Breathe in experience, breathe out poetry.

    Muriel Rukeyser, American poet and activist

A person who publishes a book wilfully appears before the populace with his pants down.
> Edna St Vincent Millay, American lyrical poet and playwright

Beware of advice – even this.
> Carl Sandburg, American writer and editor

My prescription for writer's block? Alimony – the world's greatest muse.
> Dick Schaap, American sportswriter and author

I'm all in favor of keeping dangerous weapons out of the hands of fools. Let's start with typewriters.
> Solomon Short, fictional curmudgeon

The wastebasket is a writer's best friend.
> Isaac Bashevis Singer, Polish-born Jewish-American author

When I was a little boy, they called me a liar, but now that I am grown up, they call me a writer.
> Isaac Bashevis Singer, 1986

Alexander Woollcott says good writers should never use the word 'very'. Nuts to Alexander Woollcott.
> H. Allen Smith, American journalist and humorist

There's nothing to writing. All you do is sit down at a typewriter and open a vein.
> Red Smith, American sports columnist

In composing, as a general rule, run your pen through every other word you have written; you have no idea what vigour it will give to your style.

    Sydney Smith, English wit and clergyman

Writing a play is like smashing that [glass] ashtray, filming it in slow motion, and then running the film in reverse, so that the fragments of rubble appear to fly together. You start – or at least I start – with the rubble.

    Tom Stoppard, cited in K. Tynan, *Show People: Profiles in Entertainment* (1980)

Not a wasted word. This has been a main point to my literary thinking all my life.

    Hunter S. Thompson, American 'Gonzo' journalist

There is only one plot – things are not what they seem.

    Jim Thompson, American author and screenwriter

Three hours a day will produce as much as a man ought to write.

    Anthony Trollope, *Thackeray* (1879)

Substitute 'damn' every time you're inclined to write 'very'. Your editor will delete it and the writing will be just as it should be.

    Mark Twain, American author and humorist

Write without pay until somebody offers pay; if nobody offers within three years, sawing wood is what you were intended for.

    Mark Twain

The time to begin writing an article is when you have finished it to your satisfaction. By that time you begin to clearly and logically perceive what it is you really want to say.

Mark Twain

I've lived through some terrible things in my life, some of which actually happened.

Mark Twain

I notice that you use plain, simple language, short words and brief sentences. That is the way to write English – it is the modern way and the best way. Stick to it; don't let fluff and flowers and verbosity creep in. When you catch an adjective, kill it. No, I don't mean utterly, but kill most of them – then the rest will be valuable. They weaken when they are close together. They give strength when they are wide apart. An adjective habit, or a wordy, diffuse, flowery habit, once fastened upon a person, is as hard to get rid of as any other vice.

Mark Twain, letter to D. W. Bowser, 20 March 1880

The difference between the right word and the almost right word is the difference between lightning and a lightning bug.

Cited in *The Wit and Wisdom of Mark Twain* (1987), ed. by Alex Ayres

Write something, even if it's just a suicide note.

Gore Vidal, American critic and commentator

When I write, I feel like an armless, legless man with a crayon in his mouth.

Kurt Vonnegut, American writer and satirist

I never can understand how two people can write a book together; to me that's like three people getting together to have a baby. One of them is superfluous.

Evelyn Waugh, English novelist

Anyone could write a novel given six weeks, pen, paper and no telephone or wife.

Evelyn Waugh

'He's supposed to have a particularly high-class style: "Feather-footed through the splashy fen passes the questing vole" ... would that be it?'

'Yes,' said the Managing Editor. 'That must be good style. At least it doesn't sound like anything else to me.'

Evelyn Waugh, *Scoop* (1938)

Novel-writing is a highly skilled and laborious trade of which the raw material is every single thing one has ever seen or heard or felt, and one has to go over that vast, smouldering rubbish-heap of experience, half stifled by the fumes and dust, scraping and delving until one finds a few discarded valuables.

Evelyn Waugh, *The Essays, Articles and Reviews of Evelyn Waugh*, ed. by D. Gallagher (1984)

Cram your head with characters and stories. Abuse your library privileges. Never stop looking at the world, and never stop reading to find out what sense other people have made of it. If people give you a hard time and tell you to get your nose out of a book, tell them you're working. Tell them it's research. Tell them to pipe down and leave you alone.

Jennifer Weiner, American writer and television producer

No passion in the world is equal to the passion to alter someone else's draft.

H. G. Wells, English novelist, historian and commentator

I was working on the proof of one of my poems all the morning, and took out a comma. In the afternoon I put it back again.

Oscar Wilde, Irish writer, essayist and playwright

I think all writing is a disease. You can't stop it.

William Carlos Williams, American poet and paediatrician

Ambrose isn't a frightfully hot writer. I don't suppose he makes enough out of a novel to keep a midget in doughnuts for a week. Not a really healthy midget.

P. G. Wodehouse, *The Luck of the Bodkins* (1935)

I'm writing a book. I've got the page numbers done.

Steven Wright, American comedian

I almost always urge people to write in the first person ... Writing is an act of ego and you might as well admit it.
William Zinsser, American journalist, critic and teacher

#WRITERS VERSUS CRITICS

To literary critics, a book is assumed to be guilty until it proves itself innocent.
Nelson Algren, American film writer

A bad review may spoil your breakfast but you shouldn't allow it to spoil your lunch.
Kingsley Amis, English novelist

Some people think this is the worst, most banal, most puerile piece of playwriting ever inflicted on a paying audience. Others don't think it's as good as that.
Anon.

ARTIST: So what's your opinion of my painting?
CRITIC: It's worthless.
ARTIST: I know, but I'd like to hear it anyway.
Anon.

... drooling, drivelling, doleful, depressing, dropsical drips.
Sir Thomas Beecham, English orchestra conductor, 1955

Critics are like eunuchs in a harem: they know how it's done, they've seen it done every day, but they're unable to do it themselves.

Brendan Behan, Irish novelist and playwright

Some of the editors wrote rejection slips that were more creative than anything I had written. On my tenth submission to Redbook ... 'Mrs Clark, your stories are light, slight and trite.'

Mary Higgins Clark, mystery and suspense author, 2003

I make it a policy not to read reviews. Instead, I measure them with a ruler. The longer they are the better I feel.

Joseph Conrad, Polish author

If the critics unanimously take exception to one particular scene it is advisable to move that scene to a more conspicuous place in the programme.

Noël Coward, English playwright and entertainer

The day when I shall begin to worry is when the critics declare: 'This is Noël Coward's greatest play.' But I know they bloody well won't.

Noël Coward

I am sitting in the smallest room of my house. Your review is before me. In a moment it will be behind me.

Noël Coward

How much easier it is to be critical than to be correct.
  Benjamin Disraeli, British Prime Minister 1868,
  1874–80, speech, 1860

You know who the critics are? The men who have
failed in literature and art.
  Benjamin Disraeli, *Lothair* (1870)

Taking to pieces is the trade of those who cannot
construct.
  Ralph Waldo Emerson, American essayist and poet

A bad review is wonderful when it isn't you.
  John Gielgud, English actor

Don't pay any attention to the critics. Don't even ignore
them.
  Sam Goldwyn, American film mogul

I've sold too many books to get good reviews anymore.
  John Grisham, American author

Asking a playwright what he thinks about critics is
like asking a lamppost how it feels about dogs.
  Christopher Hampton, *The Times*, 1995; also
  attributed to John Osborne, English playwright

When I read something saying I've not done anything
as good as *Catch-22*, I'm tempted to reply, 'Who has?'
  Joseph Heller, American novelist, short story writer
  and playwright, 1993

Nature, when she invented, manufactured and patented her authors, contrived to make critics of the chips that were left.
Oliver Wendell Holmes, American poet and physician

His trade is one which requires, that it may be practised in perfection, two qualifications only: ignorance of language and abstinence from thought.
A. E. Housman, English Classical scholar and poet, on critics

To escape criticism – do nothing, say nothing, be nothing.
Elbert Hubbard, American writer, artist and philosopher

Honest criticism is always hard to take, particularly from a relative, a friend, an acquaintance or a stranger.
Franklin P. Jones, American journalist and humorist

I never read bad reviews about myself, because my friends invariably tell me about them.
Oscar Levant, American composer, author and actor

Nature fits all her children with something to do,
He who would write and can't write, can surely review.
James Russell Lowell, American diplomat, poet and critic

He takes the long review of things;
He asks and gives no quarter.
And you can sail with him on wings
Or read the book. It's shorter.
>   David McCord, *To a Certain Most Certainly Certain Critic*

A critic is a person who surprises the playwright by informing him what he meant.
>   Wilson Mizner, American playwright and raconteur

A critic is a gong at a railroad crossing clanging loudly and vainly as the train goes by.
>   Christopher Morley, American journalist, poet and playwright

A bad review is even less important than whether it is raining in Patagonia.
>   Iris Murdoch, English novelist

A sneer of critics.
>   Peter Nichols, English dramatist, suggests a collective noun for critics, 1974

Book reviewers are little old ladies of both sexes.
>   John O'Hara, American novelist

I love every bone in their heads.
>   Eugene O'Neill, American playwright

In certain kinds of writing, particularly in art criticism and literary criticism, it is normal to come across long passages which are almost completely lacking in meaning.

George Orwell, *Politics and the English Language* (1946)

A critic is a legless man who teaches running.

Channing Pollock, American magician and film actor

Any fool can criticise – and many of them do.

Sally Poplin, English writer

It's a terrific show! Don't miss it if you can!

Sally Poplin

The actual definition of reviewmanship is now, I think, stabilised. In its shortest form it is 'How to be one up on the author without actually tampering with the text.' In other words, how, as a critic, to show that it is really you yourself who should have written the book, if you had time, and since you hadn't you are glad that someone else has, although obviously it might have been done better.

Stephen Potter, English humorist

I never met anybody who said when they were a kid, 'I wanna grow up and be a critic.'

Richard Pryor, American comedian

No degree of dullness can safeguard a work against the determination of critics to find it fascinating.
  Harold Rosenberg, American writer, educator and critic

If it is abuse – why one is always sure to hear of it from one damned good-natured friend or another!
  Richard Brinsley Sheridan, *The Critic* (1779)

Pay no attention to what the critics say ... Remember, a statue has never been set up in honour of a critic!
  Jean Sibelius, Finnish composer

Unless the reviewer has the courage to give you unqualified praise, I say ignore the bastard.
  John Steinbeck, American novelist

I had another dream the other day about music critics. They were small and rodent-like with padlocked ears, as if they had stepped out of a painting by Goya.
  Igor Stravinsky, Russian composer, 1969

A critic is a person who will slit the throat of a skylark to see what makes it sing.
  J. M. Synge, Irish playwright and poet

A critic is a louse in the locks of literature.
  Alfred, Lord Tennyson, former British Poet Laureate

I can live for two months on a good compliment.
  Mark Twain, American author and humorist

A critic is a man who knows the way but can't drive the car.

Kenneth Tynan, *New York Times*, 1966

Writing criticism is to writing fiction and poetry as hugging the shore is to sailing in the open sea.

John Updike, American novelist

They search for ages for the wrong word which, to give them credit, they eventually find.

Peter Ustinov, *On Critics*, BBC Radio, 1952

Any reviewer who expresses rage and loathing for a novel is preposterous. He or she is like a person who has put on full armor and attacked a hot fudge sundae.

Kurt Vonnegut, American novelist

Professional reviewers read so many bad books in the course of duty that they get an unhealthy craving for arresting phrases.

Evelyn Waugh, English novelist

It is exactly because a man cannot do a thing that he is the proper judge of it.

Oscar Wilde, 'The Critic as Artist' (1890)

Has anyone ever seen a dramatic critic in the daytime? Of course not. They come out after dark, up to no good.

P. G. Wodehouse, English humorist

Don't you loathe the critics? Their mere existence seems to me an impertinence.
P. G. Wodehouse

… inkstained wretches.
Alexander Woollcott, *New Yorker* critic and commentator

Rock journalism is people who can't write interviewing people who can't talk for people who can't read.
Frank Zappa, American singer-songwriter

See also #CRITICS AND CRITICISM, #CRITICS – REVIEWS

#WRITING – ADVICE

To become a great writer, whatever you do, avoid piles.
T. S. Eliot, American poet and critic

There is nothing wrong with writing, as long as you do it in private and wash your hands afterwards.
Robert A. Heinlein, American science fiction writer

Advice to writers: sometimes you just have to stop writing.
Even before you begin.
Stanislaw J. Lec, Polish poet and aphorist

It is a great kindness to trust people with a secret. They feel so important while telling it.

Robert Quillen, American journalist and humorist

My advice to aspiring authors is to marry money.

Max Shulman, American writer and humorist

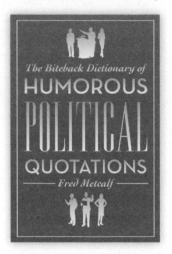

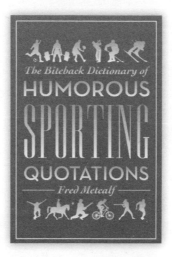

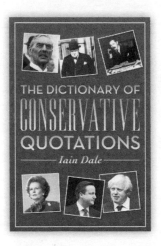

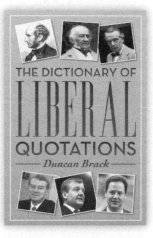

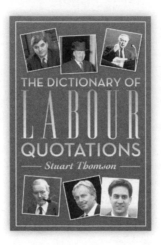